THE DURIAN CHRONICLES

Reflections on the US and Southeast Asia
in the Trump Era

Published by:
Chin Music Press
1501 Pike Place #329
Seattle, WA 98101-1542
www.chinmusicpress.com

Printed in the USA

ISBN: 978-1-63405-025-8

Library of Congress Control Number: 2022937779

Cover design: Alexandre Venancio

THE DURIAN CHRONICLES

Reflections on the US and Southeast Asia in the Trump Era

Sally Tyler

Summer 2022
Seattle

Contents

A Note on the Title

When I began writing the essays contained in this book in the immediate aftermath of the Trump election in 2016, it was primarily as a coping mechanism to indirectly analyze policy developments within the new administration while coming to terms with the travesties unfolding in Washington, DC, where I live. Adding the triangulating distance of Southeast Asia allowed me the conceit of making an intellectual inquiry that I thought was divorced from the visceral gut punch of the election. It was the only way I could do it in the beginning.

Over time, I realized that the essays were helping me understand something deeper. Try as some of us might to explain away Donald Trump's election as an aberration and act of thievery, the fact remains that he was elected president, and this says something about America that we might prefer not to admit. Likewise, my inquiry into policy developments in Southeast Asia allowed me to examine the shadows inherent in what is sometimes superficially depicted as a perpetually sunny valley.

Enter the durian. A much-maligned fruit banned from some luxury hotels and airlines because of its strong odor, the spiky green durian is still regarded as the "King of Fruit" in Southeast Asia. It is no exaggeration to say that its fragrance is reminiscent of putrid flesh.

Why then its exalted status? The taste is just as singular as its smell, but on an altogether sublime level. Cracking open the intimidating exterior reveals a delightfully creamy pod, which is the heart of the regal durian.

I first ate fresh durian thirty years ago in the state of Sarawak on the island of Borneo. Its stench permeated the market air, and I could not understand why anyone would praise this repellent fruit. But I was in a phase of jumping in with both feet, so I wanted to try it. I knew I would have to get close enough to it to endure a strong dose of its smell, but I figured I could hold my breath, taste it, earn a metaphorical badge of courage, and move on.

On first bite, I immediately understood why someone would tolerate a whiff of that overpowering smell to savor the fruit: It is simply delicious. But I was only beginning to experience the durian's true nature. Once eaten, its incomparable stink is literally internalized, as I realized to my horror. I desperately sought a remedy, downing black coffee and strong chilies, trying unsuccessfully to exorcise the smell from within me.

When you eat durian, you must accept that you will be one with the fruit for a time. True enough, modern food science has evolved to isolate the taste for a range of durian flavored candies and cookies. Perhaps it is the preservatives necessary for the particular alchemy, but these treats come off as artificial to me. Nothing compares to the unique delicacy of fresh durian. But the divine taste cannot exist without the ghastly smell. A living embodiment of dissonance.

The fruit's dual nature is reminiscent of the dissonance in the current political era. How was it possible that a nation that values democracy and the rule of law could elect as its president a man who had no regard for either? As the events of the last four years unfolded, I had to acknowledge more explicitly that the liberty and equality rightfully held up as pinnacles of American society sometimes rested on a scaffolding of oppression and inequity.

Similarly, my writing allowed me to understand that beneath the seemingly easygoing pace of life in many Southeast Asian nations was a reverence for order and conformity that made strongman governance appealing to many in the region. Those now protesting for democratic reform challenge the myths generations in the region have absorbed about needing protection from enemies without and within, which have allowed them to ignore authoritarian abuses. To achieve the degree of transparency needed to lay bare such myths, it will be necessary to acknowledge the dissonance.

Beneath my inquisitiveness about other political systems, I was buoyed by an assurance that whatever anti-democratic outrage I was witnessing abroad could never happen in America. I remember hearing a broadcaster on state-run TV in Sri Lanka, an island nation just west of Southeast Asia's demarcation, pronounce matter-of-factly that the Tamil opposition leader was a "known degenerate," and I was thankful that we had rules about fairness in the American media. When I saw legions of junta operatives in Thailand rush to reshape their Play Dough constitution to banish political enemies, I was grateful for the checks and balances in American government that would never permit such a sham. And when I talked to young people in the Philippines whose support for President Duterte allowed them to dehumanize drug users to justify their slaughter, I imagined that was how the Third Reich took hold, but never could such a distortion seize the American consciousness. The past four years have taught me that I was wrong.

As an attorney, I think I held an overreliance on the rule of law as omnipresent savior. Even the words evoke a magical power. But there is no magic. At the end of the day, the law is nothing more than words on paper without public officials who are dedicated to upholding it and a populace committed to demanding accountability of them.

These next few years, forged by crisis, will offer us profound choices.

It will not be easy. People in the US and in Southeast Asia will be inundated with challenges that ask them to hold and examine competing ideals. How can we say we champion democracy, yet only when the outcome delivers our preference? How can we say we fight for equality everywhere, yet continue to see the world in terms of competition, with our strongest motivation to avoid falling behind?

Take a beat to sit with the dissonance. And consider the durian.

1

Why Southeast Asia?*

I am a traveler by nature and a worker by upbringing. I have spent most of my adult life balancing the need to contribute and earn through work with the need to feed my soul through travel. The essays in this book are not solely about the United States or Southeast Asia, but rather about subtle connections, the way ripples on a pond reach a faraway shore. They could have been written about connections with the Middle East or Central America. But I chose Southeast Asia. Though I have traveled to fifty-five countries, Southeast Asia was where I began traveling independently, and it is where I choose to return to time after time. My experiences and the enduring friendships in the region have led me to become a student of its cultures and politics.

People have asked me over the years what appeals to me so much about Southeast Asia. I generally say that beauty drew me initially. It is a physically striking region (I hope my first view of water buffalo grazing in terraced rice paddies will linger in my mind's eye until my dying day), but I am not referring to a postcard version of beauty when I say the region's beauty draws me. Much of life there is underscored by the practice of imbuing simple actions and gestures with beauty. Look no further than the intricate arrangements of fruit and floral offerings made to ancestors in shrines along the dingiest of alleys. With intention and dedication, even mundane occurrences can be made beautiful.

If beauty called me in the beginning, strangeness kept me coming back, and

---

* *Brunei Darussalam, Cambodia, Indonesia, Lao PDR, Malaysia, Myanmar, Philippines, Singapore, Thailand and Vietnam.*

so much was strange to me in the beginning. The vibrancy of Southeast Asian street life was a captivating case in point. In my limited experience, roads and sidewalks were mere aids for transportation, while the important aspects of life were conducted behind closed doors. Not so in Chiang Mai or Phnom Penh where people got haircuts, bathed their kids, set up their stoves, and bought gasoline in Coke bottles to fuel their motorbikes, all on the street. It was a grand opera, engaging every one of my senses.

In between trips, I began to devote more time and effort to studying about the region while back home, but there is nothing like experiential learning to forge a deeper understanding. Images of the Vietnam War had been served to me as a toddler while I played on the floor as my parents watched the evening news on TV. I had grown up knowing that that conflict was tragic and deeply divisive for America. Yet, it was not until I banished my claustrophobia long enough to explore the Cu Chi tunnels on a walking tour that I understood it on a different level. Stooping down to move through the tunnels barely as wide as my shoulders, where some Viet Cong had lived for years at a time without seeing daylight, I realized with certainty how unwinnable that war had been for the US.

In more recent years, I researched and wrote about the International Court of Justice's (ICJ) decision regarding the temple complex at Preah Vihear, which had been an object of conflict between Thailand and Cambodia. Both nations claim the site, located on a mountainous stretch of border, delineated by a spurious, colonial cartography. The court had ruled that the temple resides within the borders of Cambodia but had recommended that both nations participate in a process with the goal of jointly managing the site, a repository of tremendous cultural heritage for both countries.

I wanted to see for myself, so I made the trek to the temple in northwest Cambodia along the Dângrêk Mountains, about a three-hour drive from Siem Reap. Though the Thai government had invested in new roads and a visitor center at their point of access, the Cambodian government had closed entry from Thailand following the ICJ decision. The only way to access the temple then was through the Cambodian side, from paved road, to gravel road, to dirt road, before finally heading up the steep mountain on the back of a motorcycle.

The Khmer architecture within the complex is magnificent, but in need of preservation. As I scouted the crumbling beauty of the site's seven gopuras, one of the army officers assigned to protect the site, with little to occupy him now that the ICJ decision had ended dispute over claim to the temple, allowed me to look through his telescope. I looked across the valley, now blocked as entry, into the shiny, well-appointed Thai visitor center where a family with children was using another telescope to look back at us. It was like an ironic O. Henry story come to life: one side had a legitimate right to the site but could not afford to maintain it; while the other side had the resources to invest in maintenance, yet no legal right to access the site. I had never understood the concept of Pyrrhic victory so clearly.

While in Southeast Asia, I have often found sources of education, inspiration, and revelation in surprising places.

In Hanoi, the motorbike traffic is relentless, a perpetually surging mass, with few traffic lights to stop the incessant flow. It seems almost biologic in nature, like white blood cells racing to the site of an infection. The brilliant part is that they all just go. There is no stopping—stopping would only gum up the works. As the traffic moves en masse, if a slight opening becomes apparent up ahead, the driver takes it without hesitation. There is no concern for the traffic behind. It is up to those drivers to react by bobbing, weaving, or swerving.

As a driver in Hanoi, you have two responsibilities: keep your eyes open to what is ahead, and keep moving forward. What's behind you will take care of itself. Like a lightning bolt: *What's behind you will take care of itself.* These unwritten road rules changed the way I live my life.

Time in the region, so distinct from my own, has given me much to ponder regarding my country. Travel has helped me hold up a rearview mirror to see America—the good, the bad, the frustrating, and the inspiring.

Once while in Indonesia many years ago, I was at a small roadside restaurant after a long hike, ordering nasi goreng, which would be served with salad. I asked if I could get the salad served first. I could tell by the look on the young waiter's face that it was an odd request, but he went away to ask the woman who ran the place. He returned and told me, "It is not possible to serve the salad first." The response irked me in a way that could not be explained merely by my fatigue and hunger. I was truly ticked off—not by the negative response, but by the way it was phrased. *It is not possible.* Well, of course it's possible. You may decline to serve the salad first, but don't say it's not possible, I remember thinking.

I was taken aback by my own reaction. Why was I so frustrated? Then the realization dawned on me, and I had to shake my head. *You are so American.* I had a need to acknowledge the possible in all things. Was such optimism mere naivete or was this commitment to possibility a uniquely American strength? When I think of the durian, I would say it was probably a bit of both.

There have been times when even the most ingrained optimism could not hold. After the events of 9/11, I wanted to get away from Washington, DC, which seemed to be encased by a big bull's-eye at the time. My strongest memory from that horrific day was the sunny and cloudless sky. A day for picnics and playing hooky. I have always felt guilty that I took time to notice the sky and even remember taking pleasure in the sun on my face as I struggled to make sense of the rapidly unfolding events. I paused to look at it several times throughout the day, trying to comprehend how something so menacing could have come from that clear blue expanse.

As landmarks exploded and fell, and rumors buzzed that more planes were headed our way, it came as cold comfort to hear news reports that the Speaker of the House and Senate majority leader had been whisked away by helicopter to a secret bunker, leaving the rest of us in DC to fend for ourselves with the Metro shut down and every artery out of the city clogged with those trying to escape by car or on foot.

Throughout the day, President Bush kept popping up like a mole in a whack-a-mole game, first in a Florida elementary school, then a North Dakota air base, to offer what were doubtlessly intended as solemn words of strength for a frightened nation, but what seemed like fleeting sound bites from a man on the run.

All airports were closed, and commercial air traffic was suspended for days. When it resumed, many friends and colleagues were afraid to fly. But as the weeks rolled on and still nothing made sense, I knew I needed to fly away.

I first went to Bangkok, my typical port of entry to the region, but it wasn't far enough. Thai friends kept introducing me to others by saying I had been in Washington on 9/11 and "she has great stories." Though I know they didn't mean to be insensitive, I felt too exposed to be relegated to cocktail party chatter. I needed to get farther away.

On the spur of the moment, I decided to travel to Burma for the first time. In those days, it was still possible to get a visa on arrival, albeit limited to seven days because, though the junta had decided they wanted Western dollars, they still wanted to limit Western influence. In an example of the joyful happenstance of impromptu travel, my seatmate on the flight was a young Frenchman who told me he had heard that the airport officials who collected the entry tax ($200 per person, only US dollars) could be persuaded to take a single $200 fee for us if we posed as a couple. Did I want to try? Pourquoi pas?

It worked, and we found ourselves in Yangon's humid night air with more cash in our pockets than we had expected. Did I know where I was staying? Since I had only decided about twenty-four hours previously that I was going to Myanmar (I had to remind myself to call it that, even though it was Burma I wanted to see), I had no idea about a hotel. He and I wound up traveling together that week, and we experienced a Burma that has all but disappeared as evidenced by subsequent trips. Aung San Suu Kyi was still under arrest at her lake house, billboards everywhere warned the Burmese against fraternizing with foreigners (though the slogans were written in English, making you realize the warning was actually for you), and there were daily power blackouts. It was a country that wanted to be apart. Maybe, I had gone far enough.

After a few days, we took an overnight bus that played excruciatingly loud Burmese music videos north to Mandalay. I had been able to remove myself from the events of the world for a couple of days, and it was beginning to seem like it might be possible to outrun the particular terror that had engulfed the US. Then, we were sitting in a small restaurant, and CNN was on the TV just behind my companion's head. I had not seen television in Yangon and had been able to briefly forget its existence. Now, the TV flashed images familiar to me from Capitol Hill. Back home they were debating the Patriot Act. There would be no outrunning it. I couldn't go on in denial. What was happening at home would shape the course of our nation for years to come. I knew I would have to go home eventually and find my place in an America forever changed.

But I also understood that we in the US were experiencing the fear and the loss that some people around the world lived with daily. Why should some of us be immune to that type of suffering? Is that what was meant by American exceptionalism? I spent another few weeks kicking around the region thinking on that before I went back.

Of course, I could not maintain the innocence I brought with me to the region on first visiting. Just as travel in Southeast Asia has helped me see my own country more clearly, I hope that over time I have also become a more careful observer of life there. Amidst the beauty, I have seen great poverty, political repression, corruption, and growing inequality, and I have become more attuned to the voices speaking out against it.

There have been great changes, the pace of which seems staggering when I remember the Southeast Asia I first encountered. Observations about the small and mundane can sometimes shed light on bigger questions. When I first began traveling in the region, there seemed to be no trash cans anywhere, but there was also little trash. It just wasn't part of the culture. Anything organic—rotting vegetables, bodily fluids—might be thrown into the street to decay. But the inorganic was saved—repair, reconfiguration, and reuse ruled supreme.

Now there are more trash cans, but also more expectation of trash. The region has joined the throwaway culture, even as inequality grows in scale. What could be a clearer sign of affluence than the latitude to waste?

Much as I might want to recapture the magic of my first visit, I realize that things change. I know because of Melaka.

I first went to Melaka by accident. I had been on a night bus from Penang to Kuala Lumpur that was scheduled to reach the capital city close to four in the morning. The driver was not announcing the stops, and I slept through KL and awoke with the morning sun in Melaka. In those days, I still had the freedom to travel without the confinement of an itinerary, so I just shrugged and decided I might as well check out the town.

Falling in love with a place that you never intended to visit is the quintessential illustration of serendipity. In Melaka, it seemed there were wonders around every corner—Portuguese naval officers briefly in port who asked me to share in their bacalao and Madeira, a tiny shop on Jonker Street which made exquisitely curved shoes for the mercifully few elderly Chinese women who still had bound feet, restorative elixir of watermelon juice served in the utilitarian elegance of peranakan courtyards. It was another few days before I made it to the capital.

I returned many years later, after Melaka had become a World Heritage Site and was flexing its nascent tourism infrastructure. Certainly, I had been naive to think it might remain unchanged, but the reality was dispiriting, nonetheless. The curio shops of Jonker Street had been replaced by endless stores selling T-shirts and blinged-out cell phone covers. The charming promenade by the river had been illuminated by a cacophony of neon, which made the San Antonio River Walk seem tastefully low-key.

Nothing stays the same. Even amidst the arc of thousands of years of history, Southeast Asia continues to teach me about impermanence. And this became a central benediction as I lived through the turbulence of the Trump era: This is the way things are now; it is not the way things will always be.

2

Making the Connections

Before the US presidential election in November of 2016, I contacted an associate at Australian National University who had been kind enough to review a scholarly paper I wrote and had encouraged me to contribute to *New Mandala*, a journal exploring current developments in Southeast Asia. I told him I had put together a few thoughts comparing Trump with former Thai Prime Minister Thaksin Shinawatra, drawing parallels between their status as billionaires who have avoided financial transparency, marketed false narratives as self-made men, and displayed formidable media savvy.

Like most political handicappers, I underestimated the Trump campaign and, sparked by polls that gave Clinton a resounding edge, had predicted his defeat. A few lines of my essay, however, stand in crystalline relief when trying to decipher the rise of such outlier candidates:

> *Thailand and the US are separated by thousands of miles, but base voters for Thaksin and Trump share notable characteristics. The Bangkok taxi driver transplanted from Isaan might seem to have little in common with the gun-toting, Christian fundamentalist in Oklahoma. Yet, both have felt overlooked by successive administrations and have not identified with the campaign rhetoric spun by traditional candidates. Both groups have had their votes vilified as not merely helping a disfavored candidate, but actually undermining democracy.*
>
> *Pundits on either side of the Pacific have wondered how anyone could support a demagogue like Thaksin or Trump. "What is wrong with those*

people?" was a familiar shocked refrain. The more instructive question from a political viewpoint is "What is wrong with democratic institutions for failing to craft policies and messages more inclusive of society's marginalized factions to prevent them from becoming targets of megalomaniacal candidates?" A democratic nation that ignores large blocks of voters for long will be made to pay in one way or another.

Looking back across the span of years from the vantage point of a battered, yet still standing, American democracy, I realize now that I did not fully understand the truth of those words when I wrote them. But recent history has been an apt teacher. As a nation, we chose to ignore the disaffection of many Americans in our midst for too long and recently have been made to suffer the consequences.

It would be too easy, and far from accurate, to describe the turmoil of the past four years as stemming from the actions of one man, even one with the preternatural talent of dominating the spotlight like Donald Trump. What began as a partisan screaming match morphed into a battle for the soul of a nation. Profound considerations, including the need for racial reckoning and the explosion of a pandemic that fed on inequality, only made the battle more pitched and urgent.

But Americans were not alone in noisy discourse about their vision for their nation's future, as millions worldwide, many in Southeast Asia, took to the streets for democratic reform, clear in their commitment to a collective destiny and demanding the right to help shape it.

But I couldn't see that far down the road in November 2016. My work in the US concerns both policy and politics, and post-election, I was looking for a break. I knew that Southeast Asia would afford the rest and renewal I craved, but I had not anticipated the beginning of a four-year odyssey examining comparative policies that would help me place a divided America in clearer context.

While on the road, I contacted editors at *New Mandala* to pitch an essay weaving together Filipino national hero José Rizal and efforts to repeal former President Obama's health reform initiative in the US. They liked the piece and we were off. Soon, they put me in touch with the editor of the Asia & Pacific Policy Society's *Policy Forum* who also agreed to publish my essays linking Trump Administration policy with developments in Southeast Asia.

A visit to a "prison without walls" on the Philippine island of Palawan allowed reflection on efforts to roll back Obama era criminal justice reforms in the US and mass incarceration trends in both nations. Changes to Internal Revenue Service policy in the US encouraged me to examine tax collection efforts in Cambodia, Indonesia, and elsewhere in Southeast Asia and the necessity of a strong public sector workforce to create a value-based system of tax participation. Going to the theatre in Washington, DC, to see a production of *The King and I* led me to a consideration of Thailand's lèse-majesté laws, a comparison with Trump's desire to tighten libel laws in the US, and the effect it could have on freedom of artistic expression. What began as noting quirky associations while traveling grew into a chronicle of policy reverberations between the US and Southeast Asia.

As I wrote about Trump Administration developments, an ominous theme emerged: the destructive consequences of US retreat from international engagement and multilateralism at a time when growing global crises demanded ever more cooperative solutions. I examined how US withdrawal from the Paris Agreement and the reversal of Obama era environmental regulations could give Vietnam cover for its continued reliance on coal ("Where There's Smoke, There's Coal"). As litigation helped curb the opioid epidemic in the US, I reviewed pharmaceutical companies' quest to extend their reach in Asia, where lax regulation made their dominance more likely ("Exporting Addiction" and "The Art of Pushing Pills"). And when global cooperation, robust data sharing, and shared sacrifice for public health imperatives were called for by the outbreak of COVID-19, I compared Duterte's and Trump's self-aggrandizing rhetoric that did nothing to help protect their citizens ("Strongman Politics in a Global Pandemic").

The pieces in this volume appear in the chronological order in which they were published. The diverse range of issues covered reinforces the need for international cooperation. One piece ("Reading Trump") may stand out as being less overtly political. It was commissioned as a "festive year-end read" by the *Mekong Review*, Southeast Asia's first regional literary review, for its 2017 holiday issue. It offers insights into the then-nascent presidency through the lens of literary criticism and considers the irony of a president who does not read books, preferring instead to inhabit the truncated written world of Twitter. I include it as a tribute to those who demand democratic reform in Southeast Asia because though it is important to understand the narratives of our leaders and those who act on the big stage, in the end we must write our own stories.

I have added pertinent updates to some of the previously published essays because 2021 brought a change of direction on many issues. Also included are three new articles. One compares youth-led political and social change movements in Thailand and the US and ponders what defines a movement's success. Another takes a closer look at the watershed moment for Asian Pacific American political participation in the US through the words of a diverse cohort of Southeast Asian Americans. And finally, I close the book with a dive into the challenges and opportunities awaiting the nascent Biden Administration as it attempts to steer a new course with Southeast Asia.

I hope these essays may resonate with people who believe in the strength of cooperative solutions and collective action. Individually, the essays are a series of brief snapshots over four years, but taken together, maybe they can help reinforce connectivity in what has become an increasingly fractured world.

3

Doctor, My Eyes

January 12, 2017

I recently found myself in Manila on the annual holiday commemorating José Rizal, so I decided to learn more about the Filipino national hero. A physician who turned to fiction writing to ignite the patriotic passions of the Filipino people, Rizal wrote the novel, *El filibusterismo* (or *The Reign of Greed* in English), which is now required reading for all schoolchildren there. What caught my eye (so to speak) was Rizal's chosen medical specialty—ophthalmology, which focuses on the eye and its diseases.

The eye is a wondrous chamber and, for most of us, the gateway to our perception of the world. The skill necessary to preserve or restore the gift of sight is special, and I wonder if those ophthalmologists who have entered the political fray bring any unique insight.

The effect of such insight may manifest itself in vastly different ways. Case in point: Bashar al-Assad practiced as an ophthalmologist before inheriting his father's mantle as Syria's dictator. Whereas Rizal used his vision of Filipino self-determination to inspire an independent nation, Assad has turned a blind eye to the suffering of his people, particularly in Aleppo.

In the US, the most prominent ophthalmologist-turned-politician is Republican Senator Rand Paul. His self-proclaimed libertarian principles[1] lead him to occasionally buck his party's leadership on issues, such as drones and Syria.[2] But he frequently allows any independent vision to be subsumed in favor of the party line and is a reliably partisan Republican vote.[3]

Last week, however, Paul became the first Republican member of Congress to officially break rank to say that he will not vote for the repeal of the Affordable

Care Act (Obama's health reform law) without first establishing a legislative replacement.[4] With fifty-two Republicans in the Senate, it will only take two others to join him to hand Democrats a win in the first skirmish of what will be a multiyear resistance to the Trump agenda.

Yet, the incoming president has made it clear to party leaders that the initial repeal (couched awkwardly in a budget resolution projected to add $9.7 trillion to the federal debt) will be a blind loyalty vote, setting the tone for his congressional interaction.[5] Accordingly, Senate Majority Leader Mitch McConnell is under enormous pressure to keep his people in line.

A small number of other Republican senators have now begun to publicly question the wisdom of overturning the law without a replacement, though none have yet joined Paul in actual refusal. These senators are primarily from rural states, where many of the twenty million individuals receiving health care coverage under the law reside, and where blowback to repeal, even among Trump voters, is building. Members of Congress will soon find out that once access to health care has been extended to millions of people who have not experienced it in their adult lives, a rollback is difficult.

A parallel can be found in Thailand, where Thaksin Shinawatra's opponents were unsuccessful in dismantling the former prime minister's 30-baht health scheme.[6] Try though they might to denigrate the program by linking it to the exiled former leader (much as US Republicans have always called our law by the pejorative "Obamacare"), the program proved so popular with those who benefitted from it that the notion of access to health care for all became firmly established within the Thai populace. So much so that the scheme's minimal co-pay was eventually abolished to make way for free health care for most low-income Thais.

In the US, this upcoming blind loyalty vote has enormous stakes, threatening to make twenty million Americans worse off than they were when the law was passed in 2010, when medical debt was the nation's second leading cause of bankruptcy. Additionally, the Commonwealth Fund projects that the law's repeal will cause the loss of 2.6 million jobs by 2019.

Over the weekend, Trump personally called Paul to pressure him to return to the fold, and the senator emerged from the conversation with statements that an effort to repeal and replace would be made simultaneously this week.[7] This indicates that shell replacement language may be tacked on to the budget, yet the law's scope and complexity will require months of careful legislative drafting to effectively replace. If Republicans vote for such a sham replacement, they will be goose-stepping off a cliff, not knowing whether a lake or concrete slab will break their fall.

Whether Paul maintains his independent vision in opposing repeal without replacement, or whether he will acquiesce to the demand for party unity in the new administration's first turn at bat is a major question. Certainly, as a physician, he should be guided by the principles of the Hippocratic oath. Perhaps, now is the time for all members of Congress to look to its first tenet for wisdom in this vote: First, Do No Harm.

2021 Update

The vote written about here became the first of several failed attempts by the Trump Administration to repeal the Affordable Care Act. The efforts proved unsuccessful not due to lack of fiery rhetoric calling for repeal, but because of the absolutely anemic replacement plans offered as substitutes. This weakness on policy would dog the administration throughout its term. The failures on health care were also indicative of an inability to successfully navigate the legislative process and would foreshadow a difficulty in working with Congress.

Though Trump never succeeded in repeal of his predecessor's signature law, he did use regulatory power to substantially weaken it. Such changes included a rollback of health equity and nondiscriminatory rules affecting women, racial minorities, disabled people, and the LGBTQ community. He also used regulations to eventually shutter the law's health insurance exchanges where individuals could buy subsidized coverage. The lunacy of trying to make it more difficult to obtain health coverage during a pandemic was not lost on the public and was widely unpopular. In his first week in office, President Biden issued an executive order reopening the exchanges, primarily to aid the tens of thousands who had lost employment-based coverage during the pandemic as well as to restore the critical nondiscriminatory rules.

Migration of health-care professionals has historically provided a link between the health-care systems of the US and Southeast Asia. Many developed nations, including the US, have long relied on a steady stream of nurses from the Philippines to staff their health-care facilities. For its part, the Philippines has actively promoted its role as a pipeline for well-trained nurses and has come to rely on the remittances they send back annually, accounting for approximately ten percent of its GDP.

Experiencing one of the region's deadliest COVID-19 outbreaks, the Philippines abruptly reversed this trend and began an information campaign to urge its nurses abroad to return home to help fight the pandemic. The nation's deplorable record of low pay (no pay in some instances, as nurses were sometimes asked to work full-time as volunteers) and poor safety standards left many nurses working in other countries skeptical of the pitch.

Duterte, demonstrating his typical verbal aplomb and abject indifference to his people, said health care workers would be "lucky to die" in service of their country. That rhetoric underscores what would become a global theme during a time of crisis: offering platitudes for health-care workers, yet balking at providing them with adequate wages or safety equipment.

4

A Good Day's Work

February 16, 2017

On the day of Trump's inauguration, I found myself in Thailand, a nation experiencing its own transition. As the official hundred-day mourning period following King Bhumibol's death ended, Thai people seemed anxious to get back to their usual activities.

The most visible sign of the end to public mourning was the fire-sale on black clothing all over Bangkok. The sidewalks of Sala Daeng and the pop-up stalls behind Siam Square were crammed with racks of overstock black clothing being sold at bargain basement prices, even by Thai standards. In between cruising for a little black dress at 200 baht, I sat down for lunch with a Thai labor activist associate, and our conversation turned to the government's new minimum wage policy, a patchwork of regional wage floors that has proven controversial.[1]

I asked him if anyone who was set to receive an increase was actually satisfied with the new policy. "Maybe if they live in Bangkok," he replied. My colleague hails from the still restive South, in one of eight provinces that will receive no increase to the daily minimum wage under the new policy. Seven provinces, including Bangkok and Phuket, will benefit most, with workers receiving the highest daily increase of 10 baht.

Provincial wage committees were charged with analyzing the cost of living in each province, in order to recommend appropriate increases. My colleague criticized their methodology as failing to take into account certain crucial factors. In shortchanging Southern provinces, he said analysts ignored the fact that a growing segment of Thais now meet many of their retail needs through the ubiquitous 7-Eleven, which features national pricing, not varying by region. He also said that in ranking Phuket as a high-cost province meriting the largest wage increase, analysts erred by including as part of their data sets expensive tourist restaurants where no minimum wage worker would eat.

In the US, there is a federal minimum wage, but each state is free to establish its own minimum above this rate, and many do.[2] Andrew Puzder, the fast food tycoon, who was until yesterday President Trump's nominee for secretary of Labor, has criticized efforts to increase the national wage floor.[3] Though the federal minimum wage is adopted legislatively, the secretary of Labor has a critical role in its implementation and enforcement, by promulgating rules under the Fair Labor Standards Act pertaining to the application of minimum wage and overtime provisions. The reversal of Obama era FLSA rules would likely be swift under a Puzder-helmed Department of Labor.

Puzder was due to meet with lawmakers tomorrow for a Senate confirmation hearing already postponed four times, more than any other nominee. He has now withdrawn his name from consideration as secretary of Labor. This decision came amid growing public concern about his personal and business records. Nonetheless, the fact he was even under consideration is a cautionary tale.

Puzder's CV is a familiar roadmap to Trumpland—a white male CEO with no experience in governance. His Senate confirmation hearing had been delayed at least in part because he failed to submit the required disclosure forms, apparently flummoxed by the level of transparency regarding possible conflicts of interest required of a cabinet member. Or perhaps, it was indecision on how to spin his hiring of an undocumented immigrant as a housekeeper, and the fact that he paid legally required federal employment taxes for her only after he had been nominated.

In the alternative facts favored by the new administration, his belated employment tax payment is labeled as simply a "mistake,"[4] but Democratic Senator Patty Murray offered a more pointed analysis. "[Puzder's] decision to pick and choose what laws he himself follows is disqualifying. There simply should not be one set of rules for the Trump Cabinet and another for everyone else," she told reporters last week.

The secretary of Labor's impact on domestic policy is clear, but its linkage to foreign policy has been less publicly discussed. From taking a stand on whether worker standards are included in trade agreements to weighing in on where nations land on the State Department's Trafficking in Persons report, the Department of Labor contributes significantly to US foreign policy, and decisions made by a new secretary will be felt by workers around the world.

Puzder's record as CEO offers a dismal glimpse into his take on global corporate responsibility. A key example is palm oil. Demand for the oil by the US fast food industry has helped drive tropical deforestation in Indonesia and Malaysia, contributing to global warming and air pollution in the region. As part of efforts to promote sustainable palm oil practices, the Union of Concerned Scientists released a scorecard indicating corporations' commitments to use deforestation-free palm oil. Puzder's Hardees and Carl's Jr. brands received a score of zero.[5] Because of such disregard for sustainable food practices as well as his company's sordid history of labor violations, the International Labor Rights Forum joined with more than one hundred organizations to oppose Puzder's nomination.[6]

Globally minded consumers need to know that the world's largest economy is helping ensure labor standards around the world. Just as I want to be confident that a fashion bargain in Bangkok did not originate in an unregulated hellhole like Bangladesh's Rana Plaza,[7] other Americans should be able to eat a burger that does not contribute to the erosion of habitat for diverse species in Southeast Asia. But we can't do this without a firm and vigilant Department of Labor.

Though I returned to the US with new black garb in tow, I may not need it after all. This first rejection of Trump cabinet appointments has energized those who oppose the new administration. For American citizens who care about labor standards at home and abroad, we can put away the mourning attire for now, in favor of camouflage—looks like we're going to war.

5

Lock Them All Up

March 16, 2017

The jeers of "Lock her up!" that dogged Hillary Clinton on the campaign trail because of her lax email security have now morphed into cries of "Lock him up!" aimed at President Trump as his White House is embroiled in questions surrounding possible election tampering by the Russian government. Such facile solutions may neatly fit on a placard, but when rally cries substitute for thoughtful policy prescriptions, it's time to drill down on the practice of mass incarceration and what it says about societies that embrace it.

I had time to reflect on the issue as I rang in the New Year in a Filipino prison. I was taking a break on the island of Palawan and decided to visit the Iwahig Prison and Penal Farm, a 26,000-hectare jail complex set in rural environs just fourteen kilometers outside Puerto Princesa.

Known by the PR-friendly moniker "Prison Without Walls," Iwahig strives to cultivate an image of a working farm where approximately 3,000 lightly supervised convicts toil in the fresh air in the cause of rehabilitation.[1] The reality is not so sunny. There is apparently little security concern at the prison, as only a handful of armed guards were visible throughout the compound. But there is also little hope at Iwahig.

A prisoner named Ver gave me a tour of parts of the compound open to the public (the maximum security unit is off limits). He told me that he received a life sentence, of which he must serve forty years, for selling marijuana at the age of twenty-one. He has now served thirty-two years. Ver hails from Banaue, 330 kilometers north of Manila. At the time of his conviction, he had a wife and two babies, whom he has not seen since his imprisonment. He was imprisoned in Manila for a few years before being transferred to Iwahig and says that the cost of travelling made family visits prohibitive. He says he does not think much about what he will do when he is released, as that is still eight years away and he will be an old man by then.

Historically, Iwahig has served as an overflow for Manila's notoriously overcrowded prisons, and those ranks are expanding precipitously.[2] Though most international scrutiny of Duterte's so-called war on drugs has centered on extrajudicial killings, less emphasis has been given to the ever-widening swath of humanity he has had thrown into prison. Now, lawmakers happy to do his bidding are pushing legislation to lower the age of criminal liability to nine years old, where it had been until 2006, when the age limit was raised to fifteen.[3]

Local advocates admit that Filipino drug lords sometimes use children as runners, but they counter that these children should be viewed as victims of the nation's *shabu* (meth) epidemic, rather than perpetrators. International human rights groups concur, and last July UNICEF released a statement that the policy change is against the best interests of children.[4] Still, the Duterte faction seems undeterred.

Scientific evidence regarding the pediatric brain has shown that children are not capable of understanding the consequences of their actions at a young age.[5] Such evidence has apparently not reached Pantaleon Álvarez and Fredenil Castro, co-authors of the Filipino legislation, as they posit in the bill's explanatory note that children of nine are "fully informed" about the ramifications of their actions because of the proliferation of the Internet.[6] In the US, the majority of states have risen the age of criminal prosecution as an adult to 18, and at least five more states are expected to do so this year.[7]

These laudable efforts at the state government level in the US to veer from the trend of mass incarceration threaten to be subsumed by the major reversal in criminal justice policy being pursued by the nascent Trump Administration. Through concerted approaches, including new sentencing guidelines without mandatory minimums and clemency toward individuals sentenced under previous guidelines, the Obama Administration had successfully reduced the federal prison population from 220,000 inmates in 2013 to 195,000 inmates in 2016.[8] Only days into a new Department of Justice, the dismantling of this progress has begun.

Last week, US Attorney General Sessions announced the reversal of Obama's 2016 executive order aimed at reducing, and ultimately ending, federal use of private prisons.[9] The CEOs of both GEO and CoreCivic, the nation's largest private prison companies, must have begun to whistle "Happy Days Are Here Again," as stock in both firms soared following the announcement.[10]

If there is any doubt that reliance on private prisons is linked to policies promoting mass incarceration, consider this statement from the Corrections Corporation of America (CoreCivic's former name) 2010 annual report[11]:

"The demand for our facilities and services could be adversely affected by the relaxation of enforcement efforts, leniency in conviction or parole standards and sentencing practices, or through the decriminalization of certain activities." And now, the Trump Administration has thrown the nation once again into the vicious cycle of the prison industrial complex.

The effect of this cycle on offenders has been demonstrated to be long-term,[12] as lack of economic and educational opportunity coupled with discriminatory sentencing guidelines has created a veritable prison pipeline for many young people, particularly African Americans, in the US, leaving them just as hopeless as Ver in Iwahig.

But the impact of this cycle is also felt across society. Mass incarceration of larger numbers of people for longer periods of time means that communities are deprived of the labor of those imprisoned. And it devastates families, forcing children like Ver's and countless others to grow up without a parent.

Certainly, there are important reasons for incarceration of those convicted of crimes: to protect the public, punish offenders, and provide space for rehabilitation. Depending on the circumstance, any one of these factors could justify imprisonment. But if the policy is to blindly push for mass incarceration without regard to the societal costs of segregating ever-growing numbers of our citizens, then we are all being punished.

2021 Update

The specter of mass incarceration became closely entwined with the growing call for racial justice in the US. Trump reversed Obama's ban of private prisons, paving the way for wide profit margins for the private correctional corporations that won contracts to detain the growing number of immigrants awaiting deportation. Biden outlawed the use of private prisons by the federal government in his first week in office as part of a sweeping executive order addressing racial equity.

In the Philippines, Duterte's war on drugs continued unabated. Though a precise number may never be determined, conservative estimates conclude that this campaign has resulted in at least 12,000 extrajudicial killings. In December of 2020, the International Criminal Court announced findings that crimes against humanity had been committed as part of the campaign, though it is unclear whether the court will seek any accountability on the part of Duterte.

The irony is probably lost on no one that the more bombastic the leader's law and order talk, it seems the greater the likelihood of widespread lawlessness on the part of his agents.

6

A Fashionable Entry to Policy?

March 30, 2017

This week marks the launch of Asia Islamic Fashion Week, a first of its kind trade show in Kuala Lumpur to showcase fashion featuring "cutting-edge style that is in line with Islamic values."[1] The women who wear such clothing have traditionally not identified it as "Islamic," but simply as modest. The fact that the organizers of the Malaysian exposition chose to brand it as an Islamic fashion event reflects that they are aware that such clothing, and the women who wear it, have reached a new level of global visibility in non-Islamic eyes. Though the wholesale and retail buyers targeted by their trade show remain Muslim, their work, and any messages they wish to convey through it, now includes a potentially broader audience.

Asia Islamic Fashion Week comes on the heels of last month's Fashion Week in New York, where Indonesian designer Anniesa Hasibuan, who also made headlines in September by showcasing the first all-hijab collection at the Fall New York Fashion Week, featured a cast of immigrant models in response to the Trump Administration's highly publicized travel ban targeting nine primarily Muslim nations.[2] And what could be more in-your-face than the marketing campaign for the new Nike Pro Hijab? Images of covered women who run, fence, figure skate, and skateboard flash under the caption: "What will they say about you?" Message being: the world is watching and apparently talking. Seems an unfair burden to place on female Muslim athletes—not only are they supposed to think about their technique and their split times, but apparently now, they should be equally conscious of how they are perceived by onlookers. The message is more fitting for fashion than athletics, but it comports with the overall

33

trend of high visibility image campaigns aimed at reinforcing diverse concepts of beauty to upend stereotypical thinking.

But beyond campaigns to confront implicit bias and incorporate inclusive messaging, can prominent Trump policies actually be challenged through fashion industry engagement? Lest the sartorially dismissive scoff, consider the fact that fashion is a more than $1.75 trillion global industry, accounting for at least $370 billion of spending in the US.[3] The fashion industry could potentially provide a valid test case for engagement on Trump policies because it hits on so many key issues. The complex nature of the global supply chain involved in fashion touches on trade, labor rights, gender equity, and the environment.

Last week's health care win for Democrats, and the light it shone on continued divisions within the president's own party, has set the terms for a standoff that will not end before next year's midterm elections, making it virtually impossible to achieve bipartisan participation on major issues in the near term. But it may be possible for progressive activists to remain engaged on issues of concern by backing in to policy issues tangentially attached to less controversial issues. And the fashion industry could perhaps provide such a vehicle.

An apt emissary may sit near the president, as First Daughter Ivanka Trump now has her own West Wing office in the White House. By all accounts, she is the president's most trusted advisor. She recently placed her multimillion-dollar fashion empire in a trust and will no longer make day-to-day decisions about the business.[4] But she continues to own the company and will receive payouts from it, so she will obviously remain concerned with issues that impact the fashion industry.

Southeast Asian nations could be in line for broader engagement roles on fashion industry policies. The majority of clothes, shoes, and accessories in the Ivanka Trump line are currently manufactured in China, contrary to her father's "Made in America" rhetoric.[5] Consequently, she may seek a new manufacturing base outside China, as that nation continues to attract most of her father's trade-related verbal ire. If domestic manufacturing proves prohibitively expensive, Vietnam would be a logical fallback, as a country with a well-developed textile manufacturing industry. Now that the Trans-Pacific Partnership is defunct, Vietnam is subject to bilateral negotiation with the US on trade. Such two-party negotiation could afford activists on both sides of the Pacific access to press for inclusion of issues such as labor rights and the environment. Further, the well-publicized boycott of Ivanka's line (#GrabYourWallet) that has caused US stores, including Nordstrom and Neiman Marcus, to drop her products makes it more likely that she will seek expanded placement in Asian markets.

No one should expect a public rebuke of her father's policies from this dutiful daughter, but activists on both sides of the Pacific may find traction that could be used to subtly develop positions. As one of the reportedly few climate change believers in her father's Star Chamber,[6] she might benefit from a dialogue about sustainable sourcing of textiles. And as a self-described advocate for working women, she might be willing to learn more about the impact of forced cotton harvesting on Uzbek women[7] and the effect a code of conduct adhered to by fashion manufacturers and retailers can have on women working in sweatshops worldwide.

Current political separation in the US cannot be minimized. But beneath the headlines and major issues of the day, it may be possible to engage on policy in indirect ways. When one door closes, sometimes a fashionably well-appointed window opens.

2021 Update

Perhaps, future memoirs will shed light on whether Ivanka Trump tried to persuade her father to remain in the Paris Agreement, but if she did, she clearly failed. Without evidence of moderating impact on his policies, her stature as a potential bipartisan broker quickly diminished. By the time she strode, in a smart double-breasted pantsuit, across DC's Lafayette Park, which her father had just ordered cleared of peaceful Black Lives Matter protesters by the use of tear gas, to take his side for a photo op of historically offensive proportion, it was clear where she stood. That is the image of her that will likely endure in the American consciousness and will be ceaselessly circulated if she does attempt to pursue elected office, as some have speculated.

Still, the fashion industry remains a ripe field for social activism. The year 2020 witnessed campaigns to encourage shopping at black-owned fashion businesses, increase transparency around environmental sustainability in textile manufacturing, and produce/donate masks to slow the spread of COVID-19. Asian voices have entered the mix to ensure a greater emphasis on "decolonizing" ethical fashion to show that it is far from a Western-led movement.

Social marketing campaigns should be viewed with a healthy dose of skepticism, as selling a product is always the objective. But with new legions of consumers who declare preference for socially conscious businesses and base purchasing on it, brands from luxury to fast fashion can sniff potential windfalls and will continue to showcase their conspicuous wokeness. But it won't be smooth sailing to the bank for all such conscience campaigns. These same consumers, many schooled in the rapid-fire judgments of social media, are relentless in calling out producers' tone-deaf hypocrisy, from shady supply chains to worker abuse. In some ways, fashion consumers have been more successful at demanding accountability from the industry than most voters have been in squeezing a degree of responsibility from their leaders.

As the saying goes, the hem is mightier than the sword.

7
The Taxman Cometh
(and this time, he's serious)

April 20, 2017

In Washington, DC, it's tax time, an annual rite of spring as predictable as cherry blossom season, though not quite as camera-ready. This year, the US will resume using private sector workers for collections from tax delinquents, a practice that had been discontinued after the Internal Revenue Service (IRS) determined that agency employees could do the work better. Venerable Congressman John Lewis called the new initiative a "disservice to American taxpayers" that "undermines confidence Americans should have in government action."[1]

At 83 percent, US taxpayers already lead most developed nations in compliance. But new more aggressive collection efforts aim to up that rate, and related initiatives are also meant to boost compliance. Though the IRS is prohibited from publishing noncompliance personal data about individuals, most states now publish online registries of tax delinquent scofflaws.

Various "naming and shaming" tax compliance efforts are used in many nations. In Mumbai, bands of drummers who make noise guaranteed to rouse the neighbors are stationed outside tax delinquents' homes; while in the Bihar state of India and parts of Pakistan, hijra, transgender individuals traditionally believed capable of bestowing both blessings and curses, are employed to persuade delinquents to pay up.

I watched such a woman make the rounds at a Madurai flower market a few years back. She went from seller to seller, with an energetic clap of her hands, offering the chance for either a blessing or a curse for the day. Each seller hurriedly gave her a few coins, and she went on her way. It was unclear whether the merchants simply wanted to avoid a scene or actually believed in the hijra's power to curse. Hijra have reportedly been effective at dislodging large sums of back taxes, of which they are allowed to keep 4 percent, so perhaps both levers are in play.

But the biggest boost for tax collection in India may soon come with the implementation of the new goods and services tax set to launch in July. The windfall from the goods and services tax will likely come from its "tax collection at the source" provision, requiring online retail giants, including Amazon, to collect taxes from each transaction and remit them to the government.[2] The Jeff Bezos-helmed firm is actively pushing back, claiming that the policy unnecessarily complicates the nascent e-commerce sector, but there are no signs that the government will stand down.

Thailand is also investigating tightening rules around tax collection for internet/tech firms, and Malaysia's Inland Revenue Board has recently announced a new "aggressive tax planning" office. In Cambodia, rapidly evolving beyond least-developed country status, the need for revenue has never been higher.[3] The country's speedy economic growth will likely trigger a decline in support from donor nations, necessitating even higher revenue.

This demand for revenue creates challenges to the governments involved, but it also presents citizens the opportunity to invest in the direction of the nation, and in doing so, in their own future. Such was the message of Indonesian President Joko Widodo, who promoted his tax amnesty plan to bring home money parked overseas to benefit his ambitious infrastructure plans.[4] But tax participation will only be viewed as a civic opportunity if there is transparency regarding how the taxes are spent and if individuals think they have a voice in spending decisions.

The concept of public sector accountability was sadly lacking at a town hall meeting last week in the Oklahoma congressional district of Representative Markwayne Mullin. As the congressman attempted to dodge hot questions, the audience met him with jeers of "We pay your salary." He responded by telling his constituents that was "bull crap" because the taxes he had paid as a small businessman, rather than his constituents' taxes, support his congressional salary.[5]

Funny thing about paying taxes: once people start doing it with regularity, they want to know where the taxes go, and they become increasingly empowered about voicing opinions on how they should be spent. Leaders of emerging Asian nations will face a similar reality. Invigorated tax compliance to support national growth will bring increased taxpayer demand for accountability.

Ultimately, the argument for value-based participation in a national system of taxation must be made from the top, and President Trump may be setting himself up to fall short. Almost immediately after entering office, he instructed most federal departments to prepare to cut up to thirty percent from their budgets in the form of layoffs, seemingly without understanding or regard for the myriad programs administered by the agencies.[6] Now, he has tapped First Son-in-Law Jared Kushner to head an office of innovation, which rests on the belief that the private sector can provide any service faster/better/cheaper than the government.

Trump's first proposed budget presents a conundrum. Though it includes deep cuts to vital social programs, it also features a 10 percent increase for military spending. It is unlikely that steep reductions to programs enjoying bipartisan support, such as the Special Supplemental Nutrition Program for Women, Infants, and Children (WIC) will gain clearance; so if Trump is determined to achieve increased defense spending, additional revenue may be needed in the end.

It is time for the CEO President to accept the fact that he has a new set of shareholders who expect ROI if they are being tapped for greater support. But this won't work if he is extending one hand demanding more money for the government, while using the other to give a black eye to public programs and the public sector workers who keep them running.

2021 Update

The Organization for Economic Cooperation and Development's 2020 Economic Outlook projected Southeast Asia's growth through 2024 at a healthy 4.9 percent. The organization did, however, identify a specific challenge that could slow this growth: The need to strengthen local government participation and capacity relative to disaster resilience. The region exhibits high exposure to a range of natural disasters, particularly flooding, that will likely worsen as a consequence of climate change.

Increasing compliance for local taxation will be key to meeting this challenge as tax revenue as a percentage of GDP in the region still lags behind the US (24 percent) and other developed nations with Indonesia at 11 percent, Malaysia at 12 percent, Singapore at 13 percent, Thailand at 17 percent, and the Philippines at 18 percent.

Individual tax compliance for Americans remains robust, with Donald Trump serving as a high-profile exception to the rule. For more than four decades, American presidential candidates have traditionally released their tax returns to the public, but Trump declined to do so. His legal team was still fighting subpoenas regarding his tax records as he left the White House more than four years later.

An anonymous leaker sent Trump's tax returns to *The New York Times*, which published them in September of 2020. If accurate, the returns demonstrate why the former president had resisted releasing them. They show him as a poor businessman with enormous losses who has made aggressive attempts to secure tax advantages, including setting up sham corporations to disguise millions in parental gifts, bolstering his false image as a self-made man, and undervaluing his family real estate holdings. Worse still, the returns indicated a vulnerability to foreign lenders, constituting a potential national security risk. Trump apparently paid only $750 in income tax in both 2017 and 2018, and he paid no income tax whatsoever in ten out of the past fifteen years.

This massive tax dodge demonstrates Trump's abject disregard for American government, for public sector programs and the social contract necessary to fund them. Had the returns been submitted during the campaign, more voters would have likely realized he was unfit for office. As it was, most voters had come to that conclusion on their own by the end of his term. His die-hard supporters did not see the returns as an indictment, but only as the workings of a man clever enough to outsmart the system, illustrating the profound chasm between those who value the state as a catalyst and those who only see it as an obstacle to be thwarted.

8

America First
in the Final Frontier

May 9, 2017

The verdant lawn of Washington DC's National Mall was trampled to sod on two successive weekends as tens of thousands marched for science and to call for action on climate change. Protest attire ranged from nerd chic lab coats to Leonardo DiCaprio's don't-look-at-me-I'm-just-an-ordinary-citizen newsboy cap. Outrage at the decimation of science agency funds in Trump's first proposed budget was a unifying theme, stoked by concern that his administration discounts rigorous scientific inquiry in favor of alternative facts.[1]

The proposed cuts touch on a broad range of initiatives, from critical medical research at the National Institutes of Health to standards for applying forensic evidence in criminal trials. Perhaps, most pressing for many protest participants is a fear that climate deniers are so embedded in the Trump Administration that they will force US rejection of the Paris Agreement.[2] Though a May 2 bipartisan congressional budget deal funded most science agencies at a much higher level than Trump's initial requests, the new president will have another chance at significant cuts when he releases his detailed budget in September.

Amid such well-founded alarm, it has gone largely underreported that one prominent science agency escaped massive cuts in Trump's proposed budget, the National Aeronautics and Space Administration (NASA). The overall allocation for the agency in fiscal year 2018 is $19.1 billion, a slight increase over current funding.[3] But within the agency, planetary science stands to gain a whopping 20 percent—a remarkable contrast to the budget austerity Trump hopes to impose on most federal programs.

If Trump has his way, NASA's Earth Science Division programs will be one such casualty, slated to receive a cut of nearly 13 percent from current funding levels. The work of these programs has been used to provide a foundation for evidence of climate change, and has become a favorite target of congressional Republicans and fossil fuel lobbyists.

At an October 2016 campaign rally, Trump pledged that he would "free NASA from the restriction of serving primarily as a logistics agency for low-Earth orbit activity—big deal. Instead, we will refocus its mission on space exploration. Under a Trump Administration, . . . America will lead the way into the stars."[4]

Trump has thrown support behind the notion of public-private partnerships for expanding deep space exploration, rather than relying on international collaboration. The congressional authorization bill attached to the agency's funding mandates that NASA cannot utilize space flight services from a foreign entity unless no NASA flights or domestic commercial providers are available. This could help launch US commercial flights to the International Space Station, rather than hitching rides with Russian or French rockets.

But who gets to go into deep space, and for what purpose? One such beneficiary of the change in emphasis is Elon Musk, whose SpaceX is planning to ferry astronauts to the International Space Station beginning in 2018. But it's not all official government work for Musk. He recently announced that two space tourists have placed deposits to make a trip around the moon next year in a SpaceX-propelled capsule.[5] Although Musk has said the cost of the trip is confidential, thrill-seeking high fliers have paid $20 million for a Russian-piloted trip to the International Space Station.[6] A lunar excursion could be the ultimate joyride for the billionaire boys club. Yet, while other commercial space efforts have carried legitimate research goals, space tourism flights have little value beyond the cachet of an interplanetary passport stamp, making the public underwriting of these projects unwarranted.

Trump has repeatedly called putting a man on the moon one of the US's "greatest victories" and has invoked images of Neil Armstrong's historic walk on the moon in his rhetorical quest to make America great again. Whenever I hear the name of that Apollo astronaut, I am reminded of a decades-old urban legend about Armstrong that I first heard from a Somali traveler I met in Yogyakarta many years ago. According to the tale, when Armstrong was visiting Saudi Arabia several years before, he heard the call of the muezzin urging people to come to prayer, and asked what it was. Upon being told its source, the astronaut allegedly said he had heard the very same sound on the moon, and he converted to Islam on the spot. Due to the story's spread, Armstrong was inundated by requests to appear at Islamic religious observances around the world. He was so deluged that in 1983 he worked with the State Department to send a respectful, but firm, rejection of the claim to embassies and consulates throughout the Middle East, North Africa, and Asia. But, the myth lived on through word of mouth. A few other individuals I have met in my travels over the years, generally in the Middle East, have asked about the tale's validity.

It is interesting to speculate about the story's genesis. It may be that Armstrong unwittingly gave rise to the rumor when a reporter in Egypt asked him how he found his first visit to the country. He supposedly remarked that he found the sound of the adhan (the muezzin's call) "spacey." Lacking a vernacular Arabic term, the reporter translated the comment as meaning something Armstrong had heard in outer space.

I have always been enchanted by the legend, not because I believed the conversion story, but because it underscores the essence of space exploration in our collective imaginations—a sense of awe and wonder at the beauty and mystery of the universe, coupled with a belief in the power of science to help unlock those mysteries.

This perspective—an understanding of the vastness of the universe, offset by our own precarious position in it—recently helped inform the first known political protest in space. On April 12, 2017, the Autonomous Space Agency Network attached a printout of a tweet directed at Trump ("Look at that, you son of a bitch") to a weather balloon sent into near space orbit.[7] The quote comes from Apollo 14 astronaut Edgar Mitchell who said, "From out there on the moon, international politics look so petty. You want to grab a politician by the scruff of the neck and drag him a quarter of a million miles out and say, 'Look at that, you son of a bitch'."

Others who have had an interstellar vantage point have voiced similar thoughts. Apollo 9 astronaut Russell Schweickart said, "When you go around the Earth in an hour and a half, you begin to recognize that your identity is with that whole thing. That makes a change. You look down there and you can't imagine how many borders and boundaries you cross, again and again and again, and you don't even see them."

Psychologists have a name for this enhanced sense of perspective—the overview effect. Researchers at the University of Pennsylvania are studying the effect in space travelers and are hypothesizing ways to reproduce it in the earthbound, with the goal of helping individuals become more adaptive and feel more connected to others.[8]

Although I have never been to the moon, I think that international travel has helped me develop a small-scale form of overview effect. Travel has underscored for me the essential interconnectivity of the human experience, though vastly different depending on where it unfolds, and has reinforced my own infinitesimal place in life on Earth.

Perhaps, those will be some of the notions discussed at the Asian Space

Technology Summit 2017, sponsored by Space Exploration Asia, in Kuala Lumpur. In addition to promoting space technology curricula and exploiting the untapped business opportunities afforded by space exploration, the group's stated goal is to "build the kind of infrastructure on which all of humankind's impossible achievements have been built: the infrastructure of desire and the infrastructure of vision."[9]

Since most of us will never travel through space, photos of our planet taken from deep space have helped affirm for many the notion that we on Earth play a role in the Big Picture, but are not the entire Big Picture. Unfortunately, one of the line items slated to be zeroed out in Trump's proposed budget is for the instruments on the DSCOVR spacecraft. They transmit daily images of Earth, suspended like a blue marble in the boundless universe, which have highlighted the planet's fragility for many viewers. Some have even been inspired by these images to call for a greater commitment to joining with other nations to find solutions to shared challenges, such as food insecurity or income inequality.

This is evidently not a perspective afforded by the view from Mar-a-Lago, so one can only hope that Trump rethinks his space policy emphasis, allowing what goes on beyond Earth's boundaries to inform work here. It should be a policy goal to forge ahead in space exploration, without ignoring what is in the rearview mirror. Humankind will be the better for it.

2021 Update

Space exploration was relegated to a second tier issue in the Trump Administration, with Vice President Pence tapped to spearhead a nebulous project called Space Force, intended to meld military and space capabilities. President Trump used his four years to denigrate science, particularly in relation to climate and the pandemic, culminating in an alarming press conference in which he suggested that humans could be injected with bleach to kill COVID-19.

The Biden Administration has its work cut out to reverse the damage caused by Trump's relentless anti-science posture: both in terms of achieving innovations and in restoring public confidence in the guidance of experts. On his first day in office, Biden signaled his regard for science by reentering the Paris Agreement and the World Health Organization as well as elevating the White House Office of Science and Technology to the cabinet level and appointing scientists to key leadership positions.

The dueling crises of the pandemic and economic recession make it likely that efforts to return Americans to the moon by 2024 through NASA's Artemis Project will be put on the back burner, at least in the short run. The exorbitant cost of space exploration makes international collaboration an attractive option, as fewer nations can afford to foot the bill of manned space flight on their own. Several Southeast Asian nations, including Indonesia, Myanmar, the Philippines, and Vietnam, have joined together in a so-called "super-constellation" to launch and monitor microsatellites to track weather and agriculture.

Myanmar has also announced ambitious plans to free itself from the expense and dependence of renting satellite channels from China, Thailand, the US, and Vietnam by building and launching its own satellites in the immediate future. Though originally scheduled to launch trial efforts from Japan, pandemic travel restrictions may have closed the 2021 launch window. The February 2021 military coup will doubtless make most nations reluctant to lend their launch facilities for use by Myanmar, as satellites have the capacity to monitor human activity and could make other nations vulnerable to charges of enabling human rights abuses.

Competing budget priorities may slow aggressive plans for space exploration, yet for Biden, at least, the thought will never be far from mind: One of the objects with which he chose to decorate the Oval Office, in a process traditionally weighed with symbolism, was a lunar rock.

9

Busting the
Model Minority Myth

May 29, 2017

In the United States, May is officially designated as Asian Pacific American Heritage Month, a celebration of the culture, traditions, and history of Asian Americans and Pacific Islanders in America.[1] It is typically marked by thematic exhibitions, performances, and educational sessions at universities, federal government agencies, and workplaces of some large employers.

The month of May was chosen by Congress to recognize Asian heritage because the completion of the transcontinental railroad, built largely by Chinese immigrant labor, was on May 10, 1869. The railroad fostered the growth of commerce across the US and helped secure American global economic dominance into the twentieth century.

For their efforts, the Chinese workers were rewarded with the Chinese Exclusion Act of 1882, the first law to prohibit a specific group from immigrating to the US, coincidentally also enacted in May.[2]

While there may be kimchi samplings, hula demonstrations, and anime screenings to observe the month, there will also be serious discussion of the significant contributions of Asian Americans to American culture, and how discrimination still plagues this often-overlooked minority. One such exploration concerns the Model Minority Myth and the subtly harmful effect it has dealt Asian Americans.

The term "model minority" was first used in the 1960s to describe Japanese Americans, but is now associated more broadly with all Asian Americans, particularly East Asian Americans. The term, as first used, described a gleaming embodiment of the American Dream, characterized by socioeconomic success, academic achievement, and family stability. What may have been initially interpreted as a compliment has taken on the dimension of a velvet straitjacket, trapping millions of Asian Americans in a stereotypical construct with dangerous repercussions.[3]

The most pernicious aspect of the stereotype is that it fails to acknowledge the robust diversity within the Asian American community. The sixth-generation Chinese American businessman in San Francisco is no more like the second-generation Vietnamese American fisherman in rural Louisiana than he is like the first-generation Indian American computer coder who just landed in Houston. The model minority stereotype may ultimately punish Asian Americans by suggesting their success makes government social safety net programs unnecessary—an assertion that overstates the academic/economic status achieved by some groups, predominantly East Asians and Indians, many of whom were recruited under the H1-B visa program to attract highly skilled workers, while ignoring the socioeconomic disparities that exist among some newer immigrant groups, such as the Hmong, Lao, and Cambodian.

Southeast Asian Americans may stand to lose the most if the Model Minority Myth is used as the basis for developing policy because their histories influence their socio-economic standing in ways not necessarily shared by other Asian American groups. For instance, many Southeast Asian immigrants who arrived in the US following the Vietnam War had been denied formal education due to the conflict. The impact is stark: Approximately 70 percent of Indian Americans over the age of twenty-five have a bachelor's degree or higher, whereas only 26 percent of Vietnamese Americans report the same.[4]

Poverty levels among Southeast Asian Americans are also higher, with 29 percent of Cambodians and 37 percent of Hmong living in poverty, far above the national average.[5] This suggests that some groups of Asians in America could benefit from social safety net programs.

But there is also encouraging news in that the generation of Southeast Asian Americans born in the US is beginning to reverse the trend by demonstrating a higher level of college completion.

The most in-depth instrument for measuring the demographic distribution of ethnic groups in America is the US Census, undertaken every ten years. The 2010 Census found that the Asian American population grew faster than any other racial or ethnic group in the US in the preceding decade. While Chinese, Filipino, and Vietnamese remain the largest groups of Asian Americans, the Bhutanese population in America grew by an astounding 9,000 percent during this time, with the Burmese showing an almost 500 percent expansion.[6]

The 2020 Census may be blunted, however, by severe underfunding proposed in President Trump's initial budget. While President Obama increased funding more than 60 percent in 2008 to prepare for the 2010 count, President

Trump has requested level funding at $1.5 billion, which experts say will not be nearly enough to complete an accurate census.[7]

A significant undercount could particularly impact key communities as low-income households, renters, those without phones, and non-English speakers traditionally have lower response rates. Legions of canvassers are typically employed to go into neighborhoods on foot to track down information from nonrespondents, but cutbacks will likely jeopardize their hiring.

Congress will have an opportunity to override Trump's slight of the census as the budget process unfolds, and the stakes are high, for both policy and politics. Policymakers use census results to develop social safety net distribution formulae, supporting programs such as Medicaid, special education grants, and food stamps. The communities that rely heavily on these programs will be hurt the most if a census undercount affects funding for them.[8]

Census results are also the basis for congressional redistricting, making it an extremely partisan topic. Urban voters and minorities have historically tended to support Democrats in US elections, so as population shifts to cities and as the number of minorities grow, Republicans who may wish to limit their political representation have a motive to trigger an undercount in the next census.

This decennial mapping of America's changing face comes as a new survey provides context for the complex views of some Americans toward immigrants. Upending earlier assumptions, it shows decisively that the working-class white vote that led to Trump's victory was rooted in cultural, not economic, fears/frustrations. Nearly seven in ten (68 percent) working-class white Americans think the "American way of life needs to be protected from foreign influence," as opposed to less than half (44 percent) of college-educated whites who think the same.[9]

A formidable 62 percent of working-class whites think the growing number of immigrants "threatens American culture." Working-class whites surveyed may be more insular and have less firsthand experience with America's diverse ethnic landscape, as 41 percent still live in their hometowns whereas only 21 percent of college-educated whites remain in the town where they grew up.

Accurate info from a vigorously conducted census could illuminate the true snapshot of America as a twenty-first century nation of immigrants, and help to overcome stereotypes leading to cultural isolation and xenophobia. If only congressional appropriators were willing to stand up for what really counts and those who should be counted.

10

On Second Thought, You Can Keep Your Huddled Masses

June 19, 2017

On the evening of June 6, vigils were held across the US to commemorate the anniversary of the day in 1939 when the MS *St. Louis* sailed back to Europe, its more than nine hundred German Jewish passengers having been turned away at the port of Miami, denied entry by officials of the Franklin Roosevelt Administration who understood the stark reality of what awaited them across the ocean but sent them back anyway.[1] At one vigil steps from the US capitol, participants lit yahrzeit candles in honor of deceased passengers of the St. Louis, and held aloft unlit candles in recognition of the millions of refugees worldwide who have not found permanent resettlement, yet who cannot return home.

A rabbi led the crowd in both a traditional prayer for the dead and in singing Woody Guthrie's "This Land Is Your Land." Two Democratic members of Congress told the group they would continue to push back against Trump's anti-refugee views, and would fight to return the annual ceiling for refugee acceptance to at least 75,000. Invoking the image of the St. Louis, attendees pledged the words, "Never again."

Viewed through an historical lens, the *St. Louis* decision was a logical, if heartless, extension of the era's isolationist policies, but the American public's wider understanding of global realities following World War II brought about demands on the US government to create a more receptive position on refugees.[2] The mass exodus of Indo-Chinese following the Vietnam War helped further refine US refugee policy, with Congress passing the Refugee Act of 1980. The law established permanent procedures for vetting, admitting, and resettling refugees; increased the annual number of refugees allowed admittance; and granted presidential authority to admit additional refugees in emergencies. The act allowed admission of more than 200,000 refugees from Southeast Asia.

Even though refugees from the Mideast have been the subjects of most recent headlines, Asia has provided the steadiest stream of refugees into the US over the past decade. Myanmar accounted for the most refugees admitted to the US from 2006 to 2016, with Bhutan ranking third.[3]

American refugee policy was thrown into chaos following President Trump's executive order halting immigration from six predominantly Muslim countries, along with an open-ended suspension of Syrian refugee admission. Trump may have doomed his challenge of a legal injunction against the act by tweeting that it is an intentional travel ban, pitting him squarely against the US Constitution.[4] Though he seems to regard this judicial check on his power as an inconvenient irritant, it has stopped his unilateral refugee ban for now. But refugee supporters should not get complacent. In addition to Supreme Court appointment power, Trump now controls the appointments to fill 131 federal court vacancies.[5] Once the judicial system flips, there will be little backstop to guard against the discriminatory intent of his refugee policy.

His continued conflation of refugee crises with terrorist threats only confuses a public that may articulate support for helping the internationally displaced but also remains susceptible to exaggerated fears. The fact remains that no terrorist act has been perpetrated on US soil by anyone admitted as a refugee, yet Trump's first response to attacks in Manchester and London was to beat the drum for his travel ban.

This anti-refugee rhetoric coupled with his increasingly volatile behavior calls into question whether Trump's administration can be counted upon to accept the 1,250 refugees currently held on the South Pacific islands of Nauru and Manus, called for in an agreement forged by Obama.[6] Immediately following what was characterized as a terse February call with Australian Prime Minister Turnbull, Trump tweeted that the deal was "dumb." Members of his inner circle may have rallied to persuade him that accepting the terms of the earlier deal would be preferable to alienating a close ally, as Vice President Pence publicly reaffirmed during his recent Asia tour that the new administration would uphold the agreement.

At its core, the deal appears to be a quid pro quo arrangement with Australia then agreeing to accept Central American refugees held in US funded facilities in Costa Rica. Diplomats took pains to avoid calling it a trade, but, philosophical underpinnings aside, the transaction underscores the extent to which refugees are sometimes treated like pawns to be moved around a global game board.

While Trump may have little regard for refugee policy, he and his family have shown robust support for immigration at the other end of the spectrum, particularly the EB-5 visa program. The so-called "golden visa" grants an individual a green card in exchange for an investment of at least $500,000 creating ten or more jobs. Real estate tycoons, such as Trump and his son-in-law Jared Kushner, have used the lure of the EB-5 to incent investment in their developments. A recent meeting with Chinese investors, at which Kushner's sister-in-law touted both the visa program and her relationship with Kushner, has come under scrutiny of ethics investigators.[7]

While the response to refugees by the far right worldwide grows more horrific daily,[8] legitimate concerns of host countries must be acknowledged. Host nations bordering conflict states frequently have scarce public resources, yet receive the lion's share of initial refugee flow. If there is a perception, real or imagined, that refugees compete with locals for these resources, friction will result, and refugees will lose. Consider the strain experienced by Lebanon, a nation of four million that is not even a party to the UN Convention Relating to the Status of Refugees: it has taken in one million Syrian refugees with no end in sight. A rational international system of sharing responsibility for refugees should be established, and the sooner the better. If persons displaced by conflict seem a problem too complex for the world's collective will, we had all better take a deep breath to steel ourselves for the migration predicted to be unleashed by climate change in the not-distant future. Tens of millions are projected to become homeless by rising water levels. Their situation will be desperate, yet will not fit the narrow definition of refugee accepted by the UN and the US, and will require new thinking.

A global framework must be carefully considered and painstakingly crafted to capture the interest of diverse nations, but the needs of refugees remain immediate. And for them, the stakes of a failed policy are extreme. Of the more than 900 German Jewish passengers forcibly returned to Europe on the *St. Louis*, 254 were killed during the war and the Holocaust, a reminder of the dire cost of turning away individuals who have nowhere else to go.

2021 Update

Though Biden had pledged during the campaign to raise Trump's draconian limit on refugees once in office, he announced in April that the previous administration's annual cap of 15,000 refugees was "justified by humanitarian concerns and is otherwise in the national interest," and would remain.

Outrage from progressives and refugee advocates caused him to swiftly reverse course and raise the cap to 62,500, still well shy of the 110,000 limit in the Obama era. The issue of refugee policy for those who seek US protection while still in other countries has become conflated in the public consciousness with asylum policy for those who seek protection from persecution when arriving at the US border. The situation has recently been further complicated by the record number of Central American migrants who seek entry at the southern border and the soaring numbers of unaccompanied children for whom there are no easy policy answers.

In Myanmar, many thousands of refugees have fled into Thailand and India following the brutal coup in February 2021. Thailand reportedly turned away several hundred refugees due in part to its reluctance to overtly criticize the Tatmadaw military junta and because of the strain of previously absorbing more than 100,000 Burmese refugees in recent years. The question remains for the rest of the world as to what responsibility other countries owe to nations bordering conflicts that bear the immediate brunt of refugee migration.

11

Blurring the Lines Between Church and State

July 17, 2017

Customarily, the Supreme Court of the United States saves its most incendiary decisions for the last days of the court's annual session, a sort of precursor to Fourth of July fireworks. This year's explosive decision held that states could not deny public funds to churches strictly because they are religious institutions.

A deceptively mundane case concerning a competitive grant program to resurface a church childcare center's playground, *Trinity Lutheran v. Comer* could potentially impact more than thirty US states that prevent public funds from going to religious organizations, even for secular purposes.[1] The decision is being widely criticized as a blow to the fundamental tenet of separation of church and state, but heralded by religious charter school advocates, like Trump's Education Secretary Betsy DeVos, who want to use public money to pay parochial school tuition.

While the high court ruling garnered major headlines, an even more pernicious attack on church/state separation was stealthily slipped into the 2018 Financial Services and General Government Appropriations bill, which provides annual funding for the Internal Revenue Service (IRS) among other federal government agencies.[2] By reversing the long-standing Johnson Amendment, it would eliminate the IRS's ability to define "political activity" for nonprofit entities, such as religious institutions, and would severely curtail the agency's power to investigate churches that engage in political activity.

The amendment prohibits tax-exempt nonprofit organizations, including religious entities, from participating in a political campaign on behalf of or opposing any candidate. Also, while most nonprofits may use up to 20 percent of their budget to lobby on issues by taking positions on legislation and ballot initiatives, religious organizations do not have a quantified threshold for such advocacy, but must limit any lobbying to an "insubstantial" basis, which is defined on a case-by-case basis by the IRS.

This is yet another example of the swift and aggressive action taken by ideologues with whom Trump has surrounded himself while public attention is distracted by the antics of the chief executive. Trump telegraphed his intent to undermine the Johnson Amendment at the National Prayer Breakfast, one of his first public appearances after taking office. That agenda item, however, received secondary media coverage to his using the prayer event as an opportunity to slam Arnold Schwarzenegger, his replacement host on TV's The Apprentice, for lackluster ratings.[3]

The threat of taxation has been the primary regulatory mechanism in the US to shore up what Thomas Jefferson called "the wall of separation between church and state," as articulated in the Establishment Clause of the First Amendment to the US Constitution. The primacy of this concept within American society cannot be minimized. The country's founders, some who had fled religious persecution, understood religious freedom to incorporate both the freedom to practice their religion of choice as well as freedom from religion, a concept heartily articulated by Australia's most recent census where almost a third of respondents selected "no religion" as their religious preference.[4]

But without the impending stick of taxation, would churches use their considerable resources to play politics? Other nations seem to agree that they might.

In the Philippines, President Duterte aimed his gunslinger mouth at the bishops during his campaign, and some of his supporters have urged him to begin taxing churches. But one doubts he actually has the guts to pull the trigger on his rhetorical threats in a nation with the world's third largest Catholic population.[5]

In Singapore, churches are required to register as charities to receive a tax-exemption, with revenue from side business or investment taxed at a regular rate, similar to the US. Tax-exempt income is required to be used for charitable purposes or the routine operation of their ministries. Not surprisingly, the Singapore government is efficient about policing revenue owed to it, and leaders of the City Harvest Church were criminally convicted in a high-profile case for misuse of S$50 million of donations meant for charity, funneling the funds into the pop singing career of the pastor's wife as well as an opulent penthouse in Sentosa.[6]

I got a chance to see the City Harvest Church meeting hall while in Singapore earlier this year. Huge and gleaming, with overtones of a spacecraft ready to take the faithful to Heaven, it broadcasts plainly that the church is a proponent of what has been called prosperity theology. Though geography and denominations may vary, this form of religion flourishes on many continents, and the doctrine remains inviolate: By making generous donations to the church, disciples will grow materially rich, with pastors' lavish lifestyles shining a beacon toward the material wealth possible.

In the US, one of the most prominent exponents of this doctrine is Creflo Dollar, head of World Changers Church International and author of the bestseller *You're Supposed to Be Wealthy*. He also infamously asked his flock in 2014 to contribute $60 million so he could trade up to a more luxe Gulfstream private jet.[7]

Nor does Christianity have the lock on prosperity theology. Thailand's Wat Phra Dhammakaya urges adherents around the world to give generous donations as a shortcut to merit making, and is conspicuous in its accumulation of wealth. Some have argued that the junta has been targeting the temple's assets to line its own coffers, summoning images of Henry VIII's dissolution of the monasteries to pay for his military campaigns.

But, as with everything in Thailand over the past decade, the dotted line leads back to the unseen hand of Thaksin Shinawatra conducting the orchestra from across the sea, and the underlying reason that Prayut Chan-o-cha has drawn a bull's-eye on the temple is its supposedly close association with the deposed prime minister and the loyalty that many Red Shirts show for it.

The endless *Ramayana* ballet of Thaksin and Prayut aside, the failed siege of Dhammakaya[8] illustrates one peril involved in establishing a state religion: its institutions become impervious to attack by the government, regardless of the transgressions of their leaders. Thailand's constitutional requirement that its monarch be Buddhist has created a de facto state religion. Despite its litany of charges against the wat's former abbot Luang Por Dhammachayo, the junta must tread carefully in attacking any wat, even one with deep connections to political forces that threaten its existence.

Power is, and always has been, central to the struggle between church and state. In Hebrews 10:25, when instructing Christian disciples on how to set up the new church, Paul instructs them, "Do not give up meeting together." Assembly is at the heart of most religions, and this factor makes the church a potent target for political manipulation. Devotees provide a captive audience for a message. And beyond listening, what if they could be made to act? But then, what if they are co-opted by the opposition? Add the high tech reach of televangelism and you have an instrument capable of being weaponized for partisan purposes.

This is precisely the calculus that led to Trump's move to reverse the Johnson Amendment. A man who had no contact with evangelicals until he launched his campaign, he has made the facile assumption that they will be a powerful force for his reelection, so he aims to unleash preachers across the country to speak in support of Republican candidates for next year's midterm elections. But the Christian faith, like other religions, is more diverse and nuanced than can be encapsulated by his bombastic rhetoric. If his plan to encourage political participation of churches becomes law, he may well be greeted with legions of religious leaders who oppose his efforts to deny health coverage, undo environmental protections, and allow racial discrimination, and call for their followers to cast votes on those issues.

Indeed, even the Southern Baptist Convention, a politically regressive denomination that sided with segregationists throughout the civil rights era, recently passed a resolution against alt-right white supremacy.[9] Rather than the windup music box that Trump envisions setting in motion with his move to allow overt political action by churches, he may have opened Pandora's box.

But always complicating questions of church and state is the difficulty in disaggregating between religion and culture. When most people speak of what religion means to them, they do not talk as often about spirituality or an individual relationship with God as about cultural practices. Religious adherents are taught from the beginning not just *this is what we believe*, but *this is what defines us, this is what distinguishes us from others*. Separateness and division are hardwired into the very concept of world religions.

Trump attempted to foment this sense of cultural divide in a darkly nationalistic speech in Warsaw at the G-20 Summit, emphasizing the specter of otherness.[10] Hoping to rally NATO allies to help the US fend off hordes of imagined barbarians at the gates, he implored, "We must work together to counter forces . . . from the South or the East, that threaten . . . to erase the bonds of culture, faith, and tradition that make us who we are."

Rhetorically addressing the collective West, he asked, "Do we have the confidence in our values to defend them at any cost?"[10] I would remind him that religious freedom, predicated on the separation of church and state, is at the center of American values, but it is his own Administration that constitutes the biggest threat to it.

2021 Update

Though some in the Christian evangelical movement deserted Trump's reelection, it was the renewed solidarity of the civil rights movement and black clergy that proved the most salient example of religious activism in the president's defeat. Nowhere was this union on sharper display than in Georgia, which helped ensure a Biden win and then handed him control of the US Senate by electing two Democratic senators against the odds. One of the new senators is Reverend Raphael Warnock, pastor of Ebenezer Baptist Church, which was led for many years by Dr. Martin Luther King Jr.

The combination of powerful preaching in the pulpits, grassroots door-knocking on the part of unions and community organizers, and sophisticated text and social media outreach secured a Democratic victory in Georgia's runoff elections. The win has led a new wave of faith-based activists to think that cracking the Republican Party's bright red death grip on the South is possible. While the religious right's standard bearers may have reduced its agenda to the single issue of abortion, this new wave of religious activists counts poverty, access to health care and climate change as moral issues on which they expect accountability from elected officials.

In Thailand, Prayut's government, occupied with halting the growing democratic reform movement, has ceased overt targeting of Dhammakaya and declined to declare Buddhism a state religion in its latest overhaul of the constitution, even though the king remains titular head of the religion. In Malaysia, religious polarization, fed by long-standing ethnic and racial divides, helped fuel the collapse of the Mahathir government and led to the ascent of Perikatan Nasional in 2020. Expansion of the state's Islamic bureaucracy over an ethnically and religiously diverse populace continues to breed resentments that will play out in the political arena.

Even when boundaries between religion and state are clear, the boundaries between religion and politics remain permeable, at best.

12

'Shall We Dance' with Censorship or Free Expression?

August 18, 2017

A revival of *The King and I* currently graces the stage of the Kennedy Center for Performing Arts in Washington, DC. This is the same Tony Award-winning production most notable in the US for having all Asian roles played, for the first time, by Asian actors.[1] While the production has been widely heralded for its cultural sensitivity, it is seldom mentioned in US coverage that *The King and I* remains a controversial topic in Thailand, the country in which it is set.

It would be a "puzzlement," to echo the word of the musical's King Mongkut, to most Americans that this seemingly innocuous Rodgers and Hammerstein musical could be considered so offensive as to have received a national ban in Thailand. Yet, the multilayered history of Thai authorities' reaction to the play closely mirrors the modern military role in reinforcing the monarchy, and may shed light on the growing use of lèse-majesté laws to stifle dissent.

The stated reasons for the Thai government's ban, using a film-specific statute which incorporated lèse-majesté principles, of the classic 1956 film version of the musical were that it was historically inaccurate, and that King Mongkut, later known as Rama IV, was portrayed as a comic figure.[2] Those observations are accurate. Yet, the play also depicts a monarch in the volatile

1860s, when neighboring Cambodia had just come under the "protection" of France, and Britain was sizing up Siam for a similar acquisition. Through musical shorthand, the play ably emphasizes King Mongkut's shrewdness in realizing that an understanding of European ways, one of his motives in hiring an English governess for his children, could help him fend off would-be colonizers. Though the stage king supplies plenty of comic relief, one wonders whether the Thai people might appreciate the acknowledgement of the revered king's critical role in securing their nation's history of independence from foreign powers.

A closer examination of the erratic application of the lèse-majesté rule, articulated in Article 112 of the Thai Criminal Code, to *The King and I* reveals yet another puzzlement. While the musical was banned, as was the 1999 dramatic film *Anna and the King*, the 1946 dramatic film version of *Anna and the King of Siam*, featuring a miscast Rex Harrison employing a stereotypical accent that would make even Charlie Chan cringe, received no official reaction from the Thai government. This is curious, as Article 112, making it a crime to "defame, insult, or threaten the King, Queen, heir apparent, or regent," became law in 1908, and the film-specific law had been on the books since 1930.

The more robust application of lèse-majesté laws was coincident with promotion, initiated by Field Marshal Sarit following the 1957 coup, of the monarchy's expanded role in Thai public life as well as the military's justification of its prominence as protector of the royal family.[3] The Thai people scarcely knew Bhumibol Adulyadej when he ascended the throne as a boy king, but decades of public visits to the provinces and patronage of development projects helped cement reverence toward him. As Bhumibol's seventy-year reign continued, the people's regard appeared clear, even without the lèse-majesté stick, and the king even famously said in his 2005 birthday address that he welcomed criticism.[4]

Prior to the king's death in 2016, it was virtually impossible to disaggregate the Thai public view of monarchy from the widespread affection and respect for Bhumibol. Current reality requires a new calculus that Prayut and other junta leaders may find unsettling. The Thai people can hardly be expected to transfer the regard they held for his father to the new king, Vajiralongkorn, who chose to spend the majority of his adult years living outside their country. This disconnect may allow a clearer picture of public support for the monarchy to emerge.

Perhaps in anticipation of shifting public views on the post-Bhumibol monarchy, the junta has arrested at least eighty-two people on lèse-majesté charges since the 2014 coup, according to Thai Lawyers for Human Rights, with the longest ever sentence of thirty-five years recently given to a man who posted content on Facebook deemed defamatory to the monarchy.[5] Now, the government has doubled down on the threat of lèse-majesté to silence dissent by announcing that even simply viewing defamatory content may violate the law.[6]

The White House's recent post on Instagram with a photo caption confusing Singapore's Prime Minister Lee Hsien Loong for Indonesia's President Joko

"Jokowi" Widodo at the G-20 Summit attests that Trump has not chosen to surround himself in the West Wing with Southeast Asia hands, making it unlikely that he has ever heard of lèse-majesté laws. If he were aware of the possibility of such a law, he would likely hand his Republican congressional leaders marching orders to stop beating the dead horse of Obamacare repeal and pursue a lèse-président law instead.

While the slightly more than half a year of Trump's tenure has given us wildly conflicting messages, one principle has consistently shone through: The forty-fifth president of the United States cannot tolerate even the slightest public criticism. Trump's stewing over his news coverage has led him to declare that he wants to "open up libel laws."[7]

This is perplexing, as there is no federal libel law in the US. Rather, protection against libel is derived from the First Amendment of the US Constitution. Changing the Constitution is no small undertaking, yet Trump has already begun a series of judicial nominations, starting with Supreme Court Justice Gorsuch who may well render interpretations of the law destined to undercut civil liberties, including freedom of speech.

If Trump succeeds in limiting First Amendment rights, would the new standard only apply to news coverage, or would it also include artistic expression? If it's the latter, then embattled Attorney General Sessions would need to greatly expand the number of prosecutors to keep up with lawbreakers, as the nonstop circus that is Year One of the Trump Administration may have produced no meaningful legislation, but has resulted in a bumper crop of political satire.[8]

But Americans are accustomed to satire, secure in the right to poke fun at those in power. At present, it costs Americans nothing to make jokes at Trump's expense or to laugh at them. The crucial question is who will continue to cast slings and arrows if the day comes when legal freedom of expression is curtailed.

Fortunately, we have courageous examples from around the world of artists who have slyly challenged oppressive political systems. Despite efforts to clamp down on it, some of that mischief has even flourished in Southeast Asia.

I remember my first visit to Myanmar in 2001, trudging along Mandalay byroads on an evening made darker by one of its near-daily power blackouts to a garage turned theatre illuminated by a humming backup generator, to see a comedic anyeint performance by the celebrated Moustache Brothers.[9] The troupe's founder Par Par Lay had recently been released from prison, for the crime of making jokes about Myanmar's military rules that had made Aung San Suu Kyi laugh out loud.

After five-and-a-half years of hard labor, Par Par Lay was not yet up to performing. But his younger brother Lu Maw took to the stage that night to perform the famous joke about the Burmese man who had to travel to India for dental care ("Don't you have dentists in your country?" "We do, but we're not allowed to open our mouths.") as well as the slippery-fingered "government dance," characterized by picking the pockets of everyone in sight, much to the delight of the audience.

Artistic expression, whether blatantly subversive or deceptively mundane, can create powerful impressions that engender calls for change, that sometimes succeed in shaking regimes thought to be beyond the reach of public rebuke. *The King and I*, that most mainstream of schmaltzy musicals, ends with Crown Prince Chulalongkorn becoming king and vowing to abolish requiring subjects to crawl prostrate in the king's presence, a triumph of modern sensibility made possible by his father's openness to new thought. The custom, however, was revived, at the urging of Prime Minister Sarit Thanarat, early in Bhumibol's reign.

On second thought, perhaps it is a dangerous piece of agitprop, after all.

2021 Update

The current Thai democratic reform movement is fueled by a level of artistic inspiration and lighthearted creativity not seen in mass political mobilization in decades. From crop tops and rubber ducks to illustrations boldly subverting historical themes, the movement's message demands change and makes clear that its adherents have no intention of conforming.

Though the government has stepped up its arrests of movement leaders on lèse-majesté charges, the Thai democracy campaign, like other recent social change movements, is more diffuse than centralized and is nimble enough to continue even when visible leaders are temporarily sidelined. With widespread social media sharing, the artistic protest images seem virtually everywhere simultaneously and have clearly influenced the latest anti-military protests in Myanmar.

But the joyous antics of the protesters belie their serious intent and their high-stakes dance with the authorities. Most of those participating in current Thai protests were born after the brutal Thammasat University massacre in 1976 and have no actual reference for government pushback against democratic demands. In Myanmar, the military has been practicing its indoor voice for the past decade, but protesters know the ironclad repression that could be unleashed. On February 15, 2021, the military abruptly made changes to the law to allow for sentences up to twenty years to anyone who incites hatred toward the military "by words, either spoken or written, or by signs, or by visible representation."

Though President Biden quickly sanctioned Myanmar's military for its suppression of election results, there would be scant public support in the US for further intervention given the plethora of competing domestic crises faced by the new administration. The situation will likely be the focus for intensive diplomacy, a process made more difficult by Trump's neglect over the previous four years.

13

Exporting Addiction

September 7, 2017

Methamphetamine, whether called *shabu* in the Philippines or *yaba* in Thailand, has long eclipsed heroin as the most abused illicit drug in Southeast Asia, despite the region's proximity to the Golden Triangle.[1] Ironically, though the US is half a world away from opium's fertile crescent, Americans consume more drugs derived from opium than any other nation. Opioid overdoses are now the most common type of accidental death in the US, accounting for more fatalities than gun homicides and car crashes combined.[2]

Supply-side intervention led by law enforcement has been the hallmark of anti-drug abuse efforts on both continents, and, despite highly publicized periodic drug busts, has done little to stem the tide of illicit drugs.

When the US launched its so-called war on drugs in the 1980s in response to the scourge of crack cocaine, criminal justice and sentencing policies were adjusted to incarcerate more people for longer times. Now, 16 percent of all federal and state prisoners are locked up for drug use, possession, or sale, down from a high of 22 percent in 2000.

More than half of all prisoners in Indonesia, Malaysia, Myanmar, the Philippines, and Thailand are jailed for drug related crimes, and many nations in the region require compulsory detention for drug addicts. Such compulsory detention centers have come under scrutiny for human rights abuses and for lacking science-based rehabilitation therapies.[3]

But more attention is being paid to evidence-based efforts to lessen demand. In the US, the newly formed Commission on Combating Drug Addiction and the Opioid Crisis released a report[4] calling for enhanced access to medication-assisted treatment, the most promising modality for opioid abuse treatment.

Plans are also moving forward to build a rehabilitation center in every one of the Philippines's eighty-one provinces,[5] though this will surely not meet the demand of the 700,000 individuals who have "voluntarily" turned themselves in to authorities in the nation's controversial war against drugs.

Fortunately, data about the most effective methods to help addicts avoid relapse are shaping the arguments of advocates on both continents calling for more access to therapeutic treatment.

Not that you would know this from the words of leaders like Trump and Duterte, whose Wild West talk reduces the epidemic to a matinee showdown between good guys and bad guys. The Philippine president's rhetoric about the nature of addiction has been far from constructive. In response to criticism in 2016 that his war on drugs involved human rights violations, he said, "Are they humans? What is your definition of a human being?"[6] And in announcing the recent report of his commission on the opioid crisis, Trump made no mention of specific recommendations, though he twice uttered the platitude that if people "don't start abusing drugs, they will never have a problem."[7]

If only it were that easy. Perhaps, he should have first read the commission's report. It highlights that four out of every five new heroin users in the US started with prescription opioid use.

US states have passed legislation attempting to halt the rapid transformation from patient to addict by creating prescription drug databases that can be monitored by law enforcement to scrutinize, and potentially stop, over-prescribers of opioids. The efforts are working, as prescriptions for OxyContin (a brand name for oxycodone) have declined by 40 percent since 2010. But even as reforms are taking hold in the US, Big Pharma is strategizing ways to keep global sales strong. Following the "playbook of big tobacco" manufacturers, the drug companies' solution to enhanced scrutiny back home involves global expansion, particularly in Asia's developing nations.[8]

Mundipharma, a subsidiary of Purdue Pharma, the maker of OxyContin, first began operations in Asia in 2011, as US sales began to drop. With regional offices in Singapore, the firm's promotional materials downplay the risk of opioid addiction. Instead, flashy marketing campaigns have featured glamorous celebrities who tell viewers not to resign themselves to chronic pain.

The message that the affluent do not have to suffer with chronic pain is aimed directly at those poised for social mobility. Market analysts project that rapidly modernizing countries will spend more than US$20 billion on pain medicines by 2020.

Members of the US Congress have written to the World Health Organization's Director General to warn of Mundipharma's "deceptive and dangerous practices" in promoting OxyContin sales abroad. They argue that the international health community has a "rare opportunity to see the future," and urge WHO to reign in Purdue and Mundipharma "while there is still time."[9]

Such efforts must include tighter scrutiny of trade deals to ensure that pharmaceutical companies are not simply greasing a pipeline to supply addictive use of opioids in foreign markets. Public health officials in Asia must also launch education campaigns aimed at both physicians and patients warning of the danger of inappropriate opioid use. A long-term reliance on prescription painkillers is one aspect of the Western lifestyle that should not be categorized as export-grade under any scenario.

14

The Art of Pushing Pills

November 29, 2019

This essay was commissioned by the editorial staff of the Asia and Pacific Policy Society's Policy Forum *as part of its fifth anniversary celebration and as a follow-up to "Exporting Addiction," one of its most read stories of the previous five years.*

The legacy that billionaire members of the Sackler family had hoped to create through donation of renowned collections of Asian art to major museums[1] is now being eclipsed by what may be a more lasting, and certainly more ignominious, association—the Sacklers as instigators of an opioid addiction epidemic fueled by family company Purdue Pharma's aggressive marketing.

That epidemic, which has taken 400,000 lives in the US, now wreaks destruction in Australia[2] and threatens to spread throughout Asia.

In September, Purdue Pharma filed for bankruptcy as part of a settlement with states and cities suing the company for its role in the opioid crisis. Critics of the settlement claim that the Sackler family is using it to shield their personal finances from liability and note that the settlement amount would derive partly from future opioid sales, a trade-off that many find morally objectionable.[3] These future sales would come from the sales of Mundipharma, the Singapore-based subsidiary of Purdue, which began Asian operation in 2011 and already has a 75 percent market share of painkiller sales in China.

Global expansion is a pragmatic next step for the pharmaceutical giant, as the initially welcoming environment for its products in the US has significantly chilled. A recent Harvard Medical School study showed a 54 percent drop in first-time opioid prescriptions, a major target for addiction risk reduction.[4]

What's more, the nation's drug overdose death rate declined last year for the first time in three decades.[5]

This improvement in mortality, however, should not be viewed as an overall lifting of the opioid epidemic because increased use of Naloxone, an overdose-reversing drug, is a probable contributor to the decline in deaths.[6] Tens of thousands are still overdosing, but an increasing number of family members, police officers, and even librarians have a reversal drug at their disposal and are ready to take on the grim task of reviving someone from the brink.[7]

When I wrote "Exporting Addiction" more than two years ago, one reader commented that we should not be worried about opioid addiction spreading to Asia because of historical reluctance to prescribe such medication. He was right that the specter of opium addiction from past centuries still influences medicine in many Asian countries, but cultural practices change over time. The laudable goals of the nascent palliative care movement in India have helped weaken objections to easing the pain of the dying. And aggressive marketers, like Mundipharma, will take advantage of any opportunity to expand the national appetite for pain management. Now, opioids in pills, patches, injectables, and syrups are available at not just hospitals and licensed clinics, but in street corner chemist shops in villages throughout India.[8]

However, the slide from prescription opioids to illicit fentanyl use can be swift, and signs point to trouble in Asia. Production and transit of fentanyl, which can be a hundred times more potent than morphine, has increased in Thailand, India, and Pakistan. A Chinese court recently sentenced nine individuals for fentanyl trafficking, potentially a sign of greater drug enforcement cooperation with the US.[9]

Changing use trends are accompanying reconsideration of past drug policies by some Southeast Asian nations. Thailand is shifting away from incarceration to a system of voluntary treatment for some offenders.[10] In the Philippines, Duterte may have implicitly acknowledged the failure of his violent war on drugs by naming Leni Robredo, his chief political rival, to helm the campaign this month.[11]

Sound policies are needed to counter the relentless mission creep of the pharmaceutical industry. In the US, legislatures in forty-five states considered more than 480 bills related to opioid misuse and overdose in 2018.[12] Most states operate electronic databases to track prescriptions. Some states now require Naloxone be dispensed concurrent with any opioid.

Other evidence-based strategies at work in the US include access to medication-assisted treatment to curb addiction, academic detailing to physicians to counter the disproportionate influence of the drug industry, and screening for fentanyl during toxicology tests.

The Harvard study that demonstrated the drop in opioid prescriptions concluded that such an abrupt cessation may ultimately not be in the best interest of patients, as it may leave some untreated for pain. This begs the question: Why hasn't there been more emphasis on developing non-addictive pain relievers to treat severe chronic pain?

Within the past year, there has been a significant breakthrough. The new compound binds powerfully with opioid receptors, yet also blocks the unwanted side effects of current opioid drugs and is not reinforcing, making it less ripe for abuse. Researchers hope to soon proceed to clinical trials. But the pathway to market can be long.[13] Until then, those who are suffering may have few options, but they should at least be guided by evidence-based policies.

2021 Update

The lower death rate in the US resulting from the advent of medication-assisted treatment and the widespread availability of Naloxone was obliterated as the COVID-19 pandemic began a spike in overdose deaths. Conditions stemming from the pandemic, such as economic disruption, social isolation, mental health stress, and reduced access to in-person drug treatment, are thought to have contributed to the increase.

Meanwhile, a recent UN Office on Drugs & Crime report noted that while there has been a decline in heroin production in the Golden Triangle of Myanmar, Laos, and Thailand, it has been supplanted by the steady emergence of synthetic opioids such as fentanyl.

These factors will make the Biden Administration's cooperation with Southeast Asian governments on organized crime reduction even more important. Myanmar remains the biggest meth producer in the region, and the turmoil stemming from the coup in February 2021 makes it more likely that illicit drug production will increase. Ironically, US-led sanctions meant to weaken the junta may exacerbate the illicit drug trade by forcing desperate Burmese into the drug business, as paths in the formal economy are no longer viable. Further, ethnic militias fighting the junta have historically been funded in part by the drug trade. As the nation hurtles closer to failed state status, it becomes more likely that the junta may attempt to cut deals with militias agreeing to turn a blind eye to drug production and trafficking in return for a semblance of peaceful coexistence.

15

Where There's Smoke, There's Coal

October 13, 2017

U S Department of Energy Secretary Rick Perry just delivered a double dose of bad news for proponents of renewable energy. Last week, he announced that the department would provide an additional US$3.7 billion in loan guarantees to complete the stalled construction of two controversial nuclear reactors.[1] He also included a request to the Federal Energy Regulatory Commission that it adopt rules to allow nuclear and coal plants competing in regional electricity markets to be disproportionately compensated.

The commission, which has historically been fuel neutral, is now being asked to favor certain types of energy generation in its policies. If the commission adopts policy to prop up coal and nuclear powered electricity plants, then renewable energy, including solar and wind, will be disadvantaged. On top of that, grid operators will likely begin dropping renewable energy plants from their production lineup, virtually ending competition in regional electricity markets.[2]

Ironically, this blow to investment in renewable energy arrives simultaneously with a new study that concludes that ocean wind power generation can exceed land power generation by a factor of three or more. The study suggests that if deepwater wind farms were to become technically and economically feasible, which will be heavily influenced by the course of investment, they could potentially provide civilization-scale power.[3]

Perry's announcement comes on the heels of a controversial report issued by his department on the sustainability of the US electric grid. The report concluded that coal and nuclear plants are being priced out of the electricity market not just by natural gas generated through fracking, but also by the growing use of wind and solar, and the Trump Administration's favorite stalking horse—government regulation.[4]

Perry's solution is to not only subsidize industries that are proving to be uncompetitive, but also recommend that the Environmental Protection Agency ease permitting requirements for new investments in coal plants as well as urge the Nuclear Regulatory Commission to loosen safety regulations at nuclear plants. Even for an administration that seemingly cannot clear its throat without uttering the phrase, "government regulations stifle business innovation," this attack on health and safety regulations at coal and nuclear plants will undoubtedly prove unpopular, even within its base.

This week, the Environmental Protection Agency director Scott Pruitt implemented those marching orders by announcing that the "war on coal is over," and that the agency will rescind the Obama Administration's Clean Power Plan.[5] That 2015 rule required utilities to steeply reduce carbon emissions as part of the administration's overall goals to reduce greenhouse gas emissions, central to its commitments to the Paris Agreement, from which Trump has already signaled his intent to withdraw.

The Trump Administration's renewed endorsement of coal mirrors Vietnam's decision to mothball its long-standing plans to become Southeast Asia's first nuclear-powered nation in favor of coal. Citing concern over both the level of public debt needed to complete construction and "environmental risks" following the disastrous Formosa leak,[6] Vietnam's National Assembly announced a decision at the end of 2016 to halt development of the Ninh Thuan 1 plant.[7]

Instead, the rapidly developing nation has decided to pivot to a greater reliance on coal. Vietnam is projected to derive more than half of its total electricity generation from coal by 2030.[8]

This sharp increase in the use of coal will carry dire health effects, according to researchers at Harvard and the University of Colorado. Their report, "The burden of disease from rising coal-fired plant emissions in Southeast Asia," concludes that Vietnam is the Association of Southeast Asian Nations (ASEAN) country that will be most affected by coal pollution in the near future. They estimate that more than 188 excess deaths per million people will result there due to the burning of coal.[9]

With the Asia-Pacific region representing four of the world's top five coal producers (China, India, Australia, and Indonesia), significant shifts toward coal could create economic benefits in the area—but these will be more than offset by the erosion of progress toward the Paris Agreement goals. If investment in renewable energy stalls, the global objective of decreasing greenhouse gas emissions by 2030 may prove unreachable. Thus, the "Bridge Scenario" to increase Southeast Asia's reliance on renewable energy and decrease oil and coal consumption, envisioned by a 2015 report[10] from the International Energy Agency, would be largely obliterated.

The latest Trump pronouncements on energy illustrate the cynicism at the core of many of his administration's policies. Market competition is its stated philosophical ideal, except in instances where favored industries cannot keep pace, in which case, market-distorting subsidies suddenly become an acceptable recourse.

At a time when Trump's bellicose rhetoric hints at taking up arms against other nations, it would be tragic if the US surrendered the fight against greenhouse gas emissions by declaring an armistice in the "war on coal." And worse still if other nations follow suit.

2021 Update

Vietnam did well in containing the coronavirus, allowing it to maintain a level of business continuity that was the envy of many developed nations during the turbulent months of the pandemic. As the COVID-19 crisis caused traditional big coal buyers like China and India to reduce their purchases, Vietnam swooped in to take advantage of lower prices and increase its coal buy from twenty million tons in 2019 to thirty-one million tons in 2020.

A 2020 ten-year energy plan released by Vietnam articulates an intention to use more renewable energy sources, yet does not specify steps to lessen reliance on coal. It is thought that many coal plants in the final phase of construction will still come online in 2021, yet others in earlier development stages may be scrapped.

Clearly, Biden intends a U-turn away from fossil fuel dependence, as he reentered the Paris Agreement and mandated the federal government purchase electric cars on his first day in office. The rhetoric is strong, but the new administration has a significant challenge in terms of a just transition to green energy, as energy economies in the US are regional in nature, and communities built on extractive industries will be devastated if there are moratoria on the use of fossil fuel without advance planning to shift to alternative fuel and mitigate job loss. But the new White House team has foreseen this difficulty and is framing green rhetoric in terms of job gains as part of its coordinated strategy euphemistically called a Foreign Policy for the Middle Class.

The pandemic's chilling effect on industrial production and travel resulted in a decline in greenhouse gas emissions worldwide in 2020 by up to 7 percent and some historically smoggy cities, including Beijing, New Delhi, Bangkok, Kuala Lumpur, and Manila, experienced their clearest skies in years. Still, no one should be so sanguine as to expect this is the beginning of a steady trend away from fossil fuels. Historically, new energy sources have been adopted only when they are accessible, flexible, and affordable. The world's nations have not yet made the investments necessary to assure a successful transition. But the realization that governments from Hanoi to Washington have a role to play is a first step in getting there.

16

Reading Trump

December 17, 2017

Commissioned by the editors of the Mekong Review *as a "festive, year-end read," this essay examines a non-reading president through a literary lens.*

Most American presidents have been serious readers, and attempting to gain insight into their thoughts by a review of the books they cherish has become a common pastime, starting at the beginning of the country's history. George Washington dutifully read Cato, copying hundreds of his rules of civility into notebooks, helping shape what he considered his code of conduct as a gentleman and a statesman.

After many hours of reading the law by firelight, Lincoln would turn to Shakespeare. His favorite was *Macbeth*, and it seems fitting now, knowing how he was haunted by the ghosts of those he had consigned to death in the Civil War as well as his beloved son, Willie, as evocatively explored in George Saunders' *Lincoln in the Bardo*.

In more recent times, Bill Clinton upped his coolness credentials by putting Walter Mosley's novels featuring African American detective Easy Rawlins at the top of his reading list, coinciding with Toni Morrison famously calling him "America's first black president." And speculation about which bestsellers Barack Obama would take with him on his annual getaway to Martha's Vineyard reached such a pitch that the president began regularly releasing lists of his nightstand reading to the press.

It is impossible to play such guessing games with Donald Trump because the forty-fifth president of the United States apparently does not read, for edification or pleasure.

The president has stated plainly that he does not have time to read, though during the campaign, after being continually hit with the softball what-are-you-reading question, his staff released a list featuring books reflecting his favorite rhetorical obsessions: Hillary Clinton and China. The one literary title to appear was *All Quiet on the Western Front*. He has called it his favorite book.

All Quiet on the Western Front may be Trump's favorite book, as in favorite book to serve as a coaster for his Diet Coke at Mar-a-Lago, but it is difficult to believe that he has actually read it. It strains credibility that someone who reveres Remarque's deeply pacifist ruminations about the devastating effect of war on those asked to prosecute it could engage in knee-jerk saber-rattling with North Korea.

So, Trump does not have an affinity for literature. Nor apparently can he be expected to read much in the course of his job. Aides have been instructed to keep written briefings, on even the most complex subjects, to a few rudimentary paragraphs or risk losing his attention on the topic permanently. And they are advised to make liberal use of charts and graphics whenever possible because visual images speak loudest to Donald Trump.

In this way, Trump is ideally suited to govern in the twenty-first century. He is much more comfortable in the world of Instagram than the world of the printed page. And what he lacks in reading time, he more than makes up for with TV time, reportedly up to eight hours a day.

Trump's reign as the first digital era president is also illustrated by his facility with Twitter. The round-the-clock stream of tweets that started in the campaign was expected by many to discontinue once he assumed office, but his thumbs have shown no slowdown. Reporters were initially thrown by the pugnacious, garbled (remember "covfefe"?) tweets emanating from the White House. They recognized the playground insults emblematic of the campaign, but where were the official statements befitting a sitting president?

Then they realized that tweets can, and should be, considered as official statements in a Trump presidency. Policy prescriptions and overarching philo-sophical principles alike were to be doled out in 140-character missives. This is Donald Trump's narrative, and it is overwhelmingly reactive, vitriolic, and threat-ening to those who oppose him.

In future years, political biographers will mine these tweets to try to piece together their own narratives of the Trump presidency. Amidst the insults, the ad hominem attacks, and the typos, will they be able to learn much about the motivation for decisions on critical issues?

Past writers have relied on private letters and the occasional diary to write the story of a president while in office, assuming such instruments may offer more candid insight into the moral dimensions of leadership. But tweets are composed with the expectation of being publicized. Can they be said to reflect the same level of candor or introspection?

As much, and as often, as Trump comments on others, he remains slavishly attuned to what people are saying about him. Indeed, the truest manifestation of a consistent foreign policy coming out of the Trump White House appears to be support for world leaders Trump has identified as having "said nice things about me."

On trips to Washington and during Trump's first tour of Asia, leaders seemed ready to capitalize on the Nice Words Doctrine. Both Duterte and Prayut have paved the road to Trump's esteem through compliments that will probably ensure they will never have to endure a public drubbing regarding their human rights violations while he is in office.

But they should take heed, as Trump's narrative is mutable, and he is able to disengage quickly from it when he deems it no longer serves him, and pivot to a new narrative with stunning alacrity. This can be bad news for those pledging the fealty he demands but rarely reciprocates. In fact, many elected officials who risked political capital on early Trump endorsements have been later vilified and ostracized by him after daring to disagree on key issues.

Though Trump has little inclination for literature, it is tempting to think of literary novels that can serve as an illustration of his term thus far. Burgess' *A Clockwork Orange*, with its dystopian examination of the ways in which the calculated onslaught of visual images can remold the human mind and spirit, might be a contender as well as Kosiński's *Being There*, in which a man who lives in a world informed exclusively by TV is thrust into the public spotlight, where his meaningless and repetitive pronouncements are heralded as wisdom. Those who are already angling for an ending might prefer Conrad's *Heart of Darkness*, as some might find parallels in Kurtz, the figure of an isolated leader run amok; or Achebe's *Things Fall Apart*, whose tribal leader protagonist learns all too late that times have shifted and his people will no longer heed his cry to battle. But I am resigned to at least a full term, with no deus ex machina or special prosecutor in sight, so I will not speculate on the denouement to the Trump tale just yet.

Even if no one literary novel can accurately encompass the rollicking train wreck of Trump's first year, I think that most English literature majors worth their salt could recognize that Trump is the embodiment of a particular literary device: the unreliable narrator. Between the characterization of alternative facts and his penchant for outright lies, Trump's narrative should be regarded as commentary at best and always treated with appropriate skepticism. Whether the narrator believes his own delusional point of view or is actively attempting to obfuscate the truth makes no difference in the end.

As with any novel in which the reader has determined halfway into the book that there is an unreliable narrator, it becomes incumbent to view the narrator as part of the story, but not the keeper of the story. At that point, one must become a more careful reader, looking for other threads and clues along the way.

By focusing too intently on Trump, we risk missing what is actually occurring in this administration. Trump, and the whirling spectacle he perpetuates, serves as a firestorm that sucks all the oxygen out of pertinent debate, allowing ideologically-driven maneuvers to go unchecked in other areas. Case in point: most American reporters have focused exhaustively on the epic sniping between Trump and Congress, and the stalled legislative agenda, but have virtually ignored the devastating progress made on rollback of Obama era regulations that touch every area of Americans' lives.

But the story is far from over.

After last year's election, stunned and battered by the ugliness of the campaign and its eventual outcome, I headed to Southeast Asia, where I typically find the time and space to recharge. I returned the day after the inauguration, sobered by the reality of the new administration but heartened by the massive women's march and the portent of social change evolving.

This new energy has only grown throughout the year. While elements of reaction against Trump are part of this movement, the demand for social change is larger than any one man, even if he is the President of the United States.

Perhaps, activists in Southeast Asia (and those who have not yet even realized that they are activists) can find inspiration in the example. Trump, and any national leader, will always be part of the story, but will never be the entire story. We must write our own narrative.

17

The World as a Hostile Workplace

June 4, 2018

Last week, the Academy Award winning producer Harvey Weinstein turned himself in to police in New York City to be arraigned on charges of rape and criminal sexual assault. He is also the subject of ongoing criminal investigations in Los Angeles and London based on claims of sexual harassment, intimidation, and violence made by dozens of women.[1]

Certainly, the many credible allegations against Weinstein helped raise awareness about the pervasiveness of sexual harassment in the US, with more than half of working women now saying they have been subjected to harassment in the workplace.[2] His spectacular fall from the Hollywood constellation triggered the ousting of many other high-profile media figures and politicians accused of misconduct and helped build a more cohesive movement to improve laws and corporate policies against harassment. But timing is everything, and many in the US have wondered whether the last presidential election would have ended differently had it been held just six months later, as the boys-will-be-boys shrug that greeted allegations of harassment by Donald Trump is no longer viewed by the public as an adequate response to reports of misconduct.

On the same day Weinstein was arraigned, however, an important report about sexual harassment was released to little fanfare. This report titled "Gender Based Violence in the Walmart Garment Supply Chain" details the experiences of workers in factories in Bangladesh, Cambodia, and Indonesia that supply Walmart and explains the risk factors that make such workers vulnerable to gender-based violence, including sexual harassment.[3] Though women comprise the overwhelming majority of global textile workers, they seldom hold management or supervisory positions. Instead, they generally work in the lowest-wage roles of button machine operator, helpers, checkers, and line tailors. Such gendered concentration of the workforce is endemic in the global garment industry and creates the type of power imbalance in which harassment can flourish and go unchecked.

Another typical garment industry practice that subjects women workers to harassment is the use of short-term contracts, which leaves workers at constant risk of being fired. This uncertainty allows implicit threats of nonrenewal to stifle workers' ability to report incidents of violence or harassment. Further, the common industry practice of subcontracting makes it difficult to trace account-ability back to the brand. But even if workers do report harassment and it is possible to determine the link to a supplier, more than a third of all nations do not have laws against sexual harassment in the workplace, leaving more than 235 million women workers unprotected.[4]

Now, there comes an opportunity to define the problem of gender-based violence and harassment in the workplace and to create a framework for governments, employers, workers, and unions to more effectively address it. The International Labour Organization (ILO) meeting in Geneva is convening a Standard Setting Committee tasked with ending violence and harassment in the world of work. By examining both the violence directed at women because they are women and violence that disproportionately impacts women, the ILO is expected to adopt a broad definition of worker that encompasses those in both formal and informal economies and includes all migrant workers, regardless of their legal status in the place of employment.[5]

One area that could greatly benefit from expansion of ILO standards is the export processing zone, or special economic zone, prevalent in Southeast Asian factories supplying global garment industry chains. These zones are frequently exempt from labor laws and typically feature employer-provided housing, generally large dormitories where women who have traveled from rural provinces to find work in urban factories live.

I visited such an export zone several years ago in the Dagon Township of Yangon. All the garment workers I met there were women who worked twelve-hour days, six days a week. On their one day off, many of them gathered at a training center sponsored by the Confederation of Trade Unions, Myanmar to learn English and take turns working their way through software tutorials on the center's one computer, in the hope of getting better jobs outside the factory environment.

Although the law requires workers at the factories in the export zone to be at least fifteen years old, the women's faces told a different story. Most were very young. They all deserved the right to fulfill their potential and advance in the world of work as far as their initiative and skills could take them, but I wonder how many of them abandoned their career plans in the intervening years due to the pervasive effects of sexual harassment.

Whether uttered on a Hollywood back lot or on a Phnom Penh factory floor, the phrase "You better come along if you want to continue working here—don't you know who I am?" has been used to intimidate and terrorize women for too long. The ILO can now help coalesce employment-based attitudes and practices against harassment to in effect finally reply, "Yes, we know who you are, and we're not going to take it anymore."

18

Diversity or Discrimination May Be in the Eye of the Beholder

October 30, 2018

Part of the recent drama surrounding Brett Kavanaugh's confirmation to the Supreme Court of the United States concerned speculation about how the Trump appointee would rule on fundamental questions of civil rights and individual liberties. Much public and media attention focused on his potential role in undermining the right to legal abortion should the new court overrule the landmark case law articulated in the *Roe v. Wade* decision, as many observers think the high court may be poised to do. Receiving less attention, but equally deserving of consideration, are questions about how justices appointed by Trump will stand on the issue of affirmative action.

A case heard in the US District Court on October 16, *Students for Fair Admissions, Inc. v. Presidents and Fellows of Harvard College*, will likely travel to the Supreme Court in the near term, challenging the constitutionality of the use of race in Harvard's admissions decisions. Brought by a conservative political strategist who has sought unsuccessfully for more than a decade to use litigation to end the practice of affirmative action, the current case employs a new legal strategy.[1] Previous cases opposing affirmative action have featured white plaintiffs who claim they were denied slots at leading US universities due to preferences shown racial minorities, but the current lawsuit was initiated by the conservative strategist nominally on behalf of a handful of Asian American students who claim that Harvard's race-conscious policy, meant to help create student diversity, has unfairly barred them from the university.

Defenders of affirmative action claim this is an overtly political attempt to end the policy using Asian American students as a smoke screen. Many Asian American civil rights and legal defense groups have added their voices in amicus briefs filed in support of Harvard's policy.[2] Reaction to the case belies the stereotype of Asian Americans as a monolithic community, as many recent Chinese immigrants accustomed to an academic system heavily dependent on exam scores have rallied to oppose affirmative action, while Asian Americans who have been in the US for several generations tend to support the policy. The university maintains it would be impossible to make admissions decisions on academic record alone as, among the 37,000 applications for 2,000 places in the class of 2019 were more than 8,000 with perfect grades and more than 5,000 with perfect SAT scores; and that its policy of considering academic, athletic, extracurricular, and personal qualities has resulted in an increase in the percentage of Asian Americans at the school over the years in which race-conscious policy has been used.[3]

The case is being heard in the wake of a Trump Administration decision to walk away from Obama era guidance on affirmative action, signaling clear sailing for an end to race-conscious policies from the White House. The Obama Administration maintained that the goal of racial diversity was so critical for schools and broader American society that a consideration of race in admissions policy was acceptable, so long as the standards were narrowly tailored to meet a compelling government interest.[4]

In contrast, Malaysia's array of bumiputra principles favoring ethnic Malays in its New Economic Policy could hardly be described as narrowly tailored. Though they include educational affirmative action, the policies feature a wide range of preferences meant to benefit these "native sons," to the disadvantage of ethnically Chinese or South Asian Malays, even if these families immigrated to Malaysia many generations ago. Examples include discounted new housing prices for bumiputra buyers regardless of income and a market basket of government-run mutual funds available exclusively for bumiputra that average sharply higher returns than those available through commercial banks. Critics say the policies have created a noncompetitive workforce that serves as a drag on Malaysia's economic development potential as well as an entrenched form of corruption that brings hidden costs to public sector contracts without adding value.[5] Though the policies have resulted in rapidly amassed wealth for some Malays, other native Malays, particularly those in rural areas, remain impoverished and stand to be left behind in the evolving global economy.

Originally a staunch supporter of the New Economic Policy during his first turn as prime minister, Mahathir Mohamad may have shifted his views due to the urgency of providing his nation a competitive chance in the twenty-first century economy, particularly if Malaysia is to meet its stated goal of becoming a developed economy by 2020. Soon after assuming office, he charged the Council of Eminent Persons with making recommendations to amend bumiputra policy.[6]

Despite the disparate outcomes of the policies, it is unclear whether ethnic Malays, who still comprise the majority of the country, would support changes. It's a bold gamble on Mahathir's part, one that could see his surprise return to power brought down by popular defeat or him celebrating a century on the planet in a newly strengthened nation that supports both equity and achievement.

19

Strangers in a Strange Land

January 2, 2019

Most international attention surrounding the Trump Administration's rhetoric-fueled immigration policy has focused on its constitutionally dubious travel ban for certain Muslim majority nations and its failure to achieve funding for the long-discussed wall along the US border with Mexico. Escaping broad attention has been its accelerated deportation of Southeast Asian immigrants, most of who came to America decades ago as refugees.

A December 19 charter flight from Texas to Phnom Penh forcibly repatriated thirty-six Cambodians, making 2018 a record-breaking year for Cambodian deportations. Though attempts to deport Cambodian refugees who committed crimes in the US began in 2002 under George W. Bush and were continued under the Obama Administration, Cambodia routinely refused to accept the detainees and the US did not press its case, perhaps in tacit acknowledgement of the role its covert bombing of Cambodia played in allowing the proliferation of the Khmer Rouge, the scourge from which most refugees had fled.

The Trump Administration, not known to be burdened by a long view of history, decided to prioritize the deportations and refused admission to the US of high-level Cambodian diplomats and their families in 2017 until the Cambodian government relented and began accepting detainees. The nations of Vietnam and Laos had also been classified by the US State Department as "recalcitrant" because of their similar refusal to accept detainees, but a prior diplomatic agreement that provided protection for those who had arrived from Vietnam before 1995 made it unlikely that those detainees would face deportation.

The Trump Administration met with Vietnamese officials last month to pressure them into reinterpreting the agreement to allow for the commencement of large-scale deportations, putting thousands at risk.[1]

The circumstances of those being deported underscore the senseless nature of the policy. Though most of the detainees were convicted of a felony in the US, many committed their crime as teens and did not receive a trial, agreeing to plead guilty in exchange for a lesser sentence, not realizing that a plea would make them automatically eligible for removal to their home country under US law.[2] After completing their sentences, most set out to build productive lives with the threat of deportation vague and distant due to Cambodia's refusal to accept repatriation. The majority became employed, raised families, and were economic mainstays for parents and older relatives. Now, the looming specter of deportation creates both economic and emotional hardship in Cambodian communities throughout the US.

Another layer of tragic irony is how utterly unprepared these individuals are for reentry to Cambodia. Having grown up considering themselves American, few speak, read, or write Khmer. Many have literally never set foot on Cambodian soil, having been born in Thai refugee camps before their migration to the US. Most of the detainees no longer have family members in the country, as relatives who remained in Cambodia may not have survived the era of Khmer Rouge atrocities. Without knowledge of the language or culture, and without families to help them, these individuals have a bleak plight. An American protestant minister has formed a shoestring organization with the goal of assisting their assimilation and relocation, but deportees report to their families in the US that they are isolated and adrift. A handful has succumbed to drugs or suicide.

There has been pushback to the deportations, with governors of the states of California and Washington issuing pardons to nullify some of the offenses on which the deportations are based. Still, these isolated political maneuvers continue to face legal hurdles and are dwarfed by the enhanced deportation machine of the reinvigorated Immigration and Customs Enforcement agency under Trump.[3]

The final irony for the detainees is that the conditions that gave rise to their refugee status have also made them vulnerable to deportation. Many Cambodians who survived the horrors of the Khmer Rouge understandably became wary of any government and shunned political participation as a one-way ticket to persecution. They instilled the same belief in their children, so most current detainees did not attempt to become US citizens when they were eligible. As noncitizens they have little recourse to fight deportation and as nonvoters they may not attract the support of elected officials who could champion their cause.

This political detachment is gradually eroding, however, as a new generation of Cambodian Americans is helping to educate their communities about the importance of civic engagement.[4] Perhaps greater political participation will allow affected individuals to advocate for themselves more effectively and cease being treated as pawns in a high-stakes game of chess among nations over who is responsible for the world's refugees.

2021 Update

Immigration was yet another area where Trump's outsized rhetoric was not backed up by substantive policy over the course of his term. Despite campaign promises prioritizing it, he never released a comprehensive immigration reform plan. But he did lob several incendiary executive orders in the direction of immigrants, including the travel ban targeting primarily Muslim countries and the third country asylum rule attempting to thwart overland asylum seekers from Latin America. Both those orders were reversed by Biden on his first day in office.

Forced repatriation to Cambodia gained steam during Trump's term, increasing by 279 percent from 2017 to 2019, according to the US Immigration and Customs Enforcement. By signing the earlier bilateral agreement, the Cambodian government was forced to continue accepting deportees. Cambodia made it no secret that it wants to renegotiate the repatriation agreement, but the Trump Administration refused. There is no early word on whether the new Biden Administration will come to the table.

As of February 2021, four of the repatriated Cambodians whose attorneys claim were falsely removed from the US have been allowed to return.

20

If Hong Kong Can Have Democracy, Then Why Not the US?

December 19, 2019

Though Hong Kong is not in Southeast Asia, I include this essay because the democracy movement there was critical to the Milk Tea Alliance that spurred protests for democratic reform in Thailand. It also helps illustrate the democratic reform work still needed in the US.

The November 24, 2019 Hong Kong elections sent a powerful message that its citizens demand democracy and the right to self-determination. The 71 percent of Hong Kong voters who turned out—an all-time high—made clear that universal suffrage and the right to participate in representative government is the gauntlet they have thrown down to Beijing.

US support for democratic strides in Hong Kong is firm. The Hong Kong Human Rights and Democracy Act of 2019 passed unanimously in both the House and Senate, and though he had previously been noncommittal about the bill, President Trump signed it into law on November 27, following urging from Republican leaders.[1,2] The law requires the State Department to conduct an annual review of whether Hong Kong's ongoing political relationship with Beijing continues to justify its favored trade status with the US and gives the president power to invoke targeted sanctions for human rights violations there.

The law's text states that it is US policy to "support the democratic aspirations of the people of Hong Kong." But is it US policy to support the democratic aspirations of those in Congress's own backyard, namely the people of Washington, DC?

Many people, including many Americans, are surprised to learn that US citizens who reside in the District of Columbia (Washington, DC) are denied the form of representative government that the rest of the nation enjoys. The District is not considered a state and is only represented in Congress by a nonvoting delegate and no senators.[3] Thus, the nearly 700,000 individuals who reside in the nation's capital are shut out of many of the most pressing policy decisions affecting them. This, despite paying one of the highest federal per capita tax rates in the nation, giving rise to the official slogan on the license plates of District residents: Taxation Without Representation.

On November 26, mere days after the heralded Hong Kong election results, a federal case, *Castañon v. United States*, was argued in Washington, DC, to little notice. The case argues that the right to vote for legislative representation is a fundamental right and that District residents have been harmed by their lack of voting representation as it denies them equal protection and due process.[4]

This judicial quest for voting rights is accompanied by a legislative push for DC statehood. HR 51, the DC Admission Act, has 224 cosponsors in the House, all Democrats. Indeed, the debate for DC statehood falls along strict partisan lines, with Republicans loath to support a measure that would assuredly deliver additional Democratic votes in Congress.[5] Over the years, Republican majorities in Congress have overruled the District Council when it tried to use the District's own funds to pay for abortion services for low-income women, establish a needle exchange program, and legalize marijuana.

In one of the more cynical maneuvers in recent congressional history, Republicans announced in 2009 that they would back DC statehood legislation and then amended the bill to prohibit gun control in the District, a sacrosanct issue for DC residents and local lawmakers that they knew would constitute a poison pill for Democrats in Congress.[6]

Beyond the stark dimensions of partisan divide, there is an even uglier reality to Republican denial of voting rights for DC. Forty-six percent of District residents are Black, and many analysts have clearly demonstrated the racist roots of this attempt to suppress African American political participation.[7]

But there are glimmers of hope on the horizon. In September, DC statehood legislation was given its first congressional committee hearing in more than twenty-five years.[8] Nationally respected advocacy groups, including the American Civil Liberties Union and the League of Women Voters, filed amicus briefs in support of Castañon. A dogged voting rights movement has launched a sort of pen pal initiative to link DC residents with citizens in states around the nation to educate them about the lack of representation in the District and to urge them to lobby their own members of Congress to vote for DC statehood.

While other countries with federal systems like the US may see the wisdom in carving out a separate federal district, they have also recognized the importance of representative government for residents of those districts. In the Asia-Pacific region, Australia, India, Malaysia, and Pakistan elect voting members to their national assemblies from their capital territories.

Perhaps, the bold actions of the people of Hong Kong in pursuit of democracy will inspire activists in the US. Before long, maybe we will see the motto: Liberate DC, the Revolution of Our Times.

21

Strongman Politics in a Crisis

April 3, 2020

L ike many people on the planet, I am at home, hiding from an invisible pathogen stealthier than any terrorist attack. The COVID-19 pandemic represents an unprecedented global challenge to health care infrastructures, economic resiliency, and leadership. Decisions by national leaders cast in stark relief those who view the crisis as a threat to their personal brand and those who are ready to meet the challenge through the painstakingly lackluster, if deadly serious, business of governance.

Singapore's response to the crisis has received much acclaim, and its aggressive campaign of contact tracing and widespread testing is seen as the gold standard for virus containment.[1] The city-state's response was notable in its use of public health experts as the official messengers about the national campaign.

This is in sharp contrast to the US, where Trump has assumed the role of daily explainer-in-chief, first by denying that the novel coronavirus was even as serious as the flu and later by blaming the spread of the virus on both the Chinese government and his Democratic opponents in Congress. Anthony Fauci, longtime director of the National Institute of Allergy and Infectious Disease, has had his hands full on a daily basis trying to clarify or cancel the near-constant stream of misinformation emanating from the president.[2]

Meanwhile in the Philippines, Duterte's deadly delay in implementing testing was followed by an abrupt decision to lock down the Manila region, without guidance to the capital's twelve million inhabitants about which services, if any, would still be available to them.[3] Most recently, his successful demand for emergency powers stopped short of nationalizing private companies as he originally wanted, but has nonetheless alarmed human rights critics because of the scope of his grab.[4]

Similar concerns have been voiced about Prayut's further clampdown on free speech during the pandemic in Thailand following the arrest under Section 14(2) of the Computer-Related Crime Act of a Thai man who had just returned to Bangkok from abroad and had posted online that virus screening was not being conducted at the international airport. Opponents have long been vocal about the government's attempts to criminalize any criticism of it, and many are worried that the public health emergency will be used as a cover for more repressive action.[5]

These disparate actions taken at the national level highlight the very real differences between the art of campaigning and the reality of governing. Campaigning rewards glib sound bites, larger-than-life posturing, and the refusal to admit not knowing anything. In governance, such behavior can get you, or at least several thousand of your nation's citizens, killed.

The plethora of critical issues facing contemporary world leaders underscores the importance of assembling a team of experts before Day One of a new administration and creating an effective mechanism for consultation. A prime example would be the decision-making style of Trump's predecessor, "No Drama" Obama, who was known for being comfortable with not having an immediate answer to a complex problem, but who sought out the advice of those who knew more on the subject, including those who disagreed with him.[6]

Hopefully, leaders will have the foresight to consult with other nations, as the virus knows no borders. Robust international data sharing is one of the few hopes to slow its spread. Nations lacking in transparency or who try to manipulate the evidence of the pandemic in their midst will surely endanger their own citizens and possibly the world's.

And once the public health crisis has subsided, a multilateral approach will be warranted to address underlying issues that the pandemic has brought into focus, such as economic inequality and worker migration, to ensure that they are not further exacerbated by recovery efforts. The $2 trillion relief bill that just passed in the US Congress excludes taxpaying immigrants from receiving stimulus checks even though they are among the most likely to be laid off from jobs.[7] In Indonesia's economic relief efforts, manufacturers will be exempt from paying income tax on workers for six months. This will come as little comfort to the Indonesian migrant workers who are trapped in Malaysia under a new movement control order and fear that they may starve before it is lifted.[8] As the US learned after the financial collapse of 2008, if relief efforts concentrate on business to the exclusion of workers, any recovery will be painfully protracted. World leaders must move cooperatively and proactively to ensure that the pandemic's impact is not ultimately dwarfed by economic collapse.

What do citizens want from their leaders in times of global crisis? They seek a steady hand, accompanied by unvarnished, yet unifying, speech, particularly if they are being asked to sacrifice for the collective good. They want to know that decisions are guided by knowledge and the will to apply it consistently. Above all, they want to know that leaders care more about the well-being of their citizens than their own political futures.

22

'Stay Safe' Is an Empty Platitude in a World Riddled by Inequality

June 12, 2020

In simultaneous occurrences, protests in the US related to the police killing of George Floyd turned violent and the Tiananmen Square vigil in Hong Kong was banned for the first time in thirty years. It is no coincidence that these events come as the world is grappling with the COVID-19 pandemic, and official government rhetoric surrounding each has been couched in terms of safety and security.

Threats to individual safety come in a variety of forms—a virus, food insecurity, a knee to the neck, a lone tank. The discerning public should look beyond a facile concept of safety and analyze to what extent the global health emergency is being used to deflect attention from long-standing societal injustice or to justify power grabs aimed at squelching democracy.

Curfews have been imposed in forty US cities with more than 5,000 National Guard members deployed in response to protests,[1] and many urban areas resemble fortresses without an increased sense of security for the people who live there. At a time when a fractured nation needs leaders to listen more than pontificate, President Trump tweeted an ominous "when the looting starts, the shooting starts" dog whistle to the segregationist past.[2] Such comments were reminiscent of the Philippines' Duterte when he instructed the police and military to shoot dead any violators of his coronavirus lockdown in Manila.[3]

Trump followed up by threatening the unprecedented use of military power against the American people and then, apparently frustrated at the proliferation of protests around the nation, attempted to bully governors into using force in their states by calling them "weak."[4] In both cases, Trump and Duterte made threats against their own citizens under the guise of keeping them safe.

US police and state officials have uniformly acknowledged the right to protest and have made small numbers of arrests relative to the overall number of protesters. In Minneapolis, the site of Floyd's murder and origination of the protests, officials repeatedly made the public claim that the violence was the work of outside agitators. Although there is indication that white supremacists posted on platforms posing as antifa activists to urge turnout and deflect responsibility for violence, the evidence from arrests does not bear out the claim that the violence was solely the work of outsiders, as forty-seven out of fifty-seven arrests on the first night of Minnesota protests were Minnesota residents.[5]

It is certainly not true that large numbers of people want to see businesses in their own communities destroyed, but it is misleading and simplistic to say that no local actors have been involved. Historically, the blanket charge of outside agitation has been used to mask real issues of dissent, and we should be critical in this case, particularly if it is used to minimize underlying issues fomenting unrest.

Individuals who participate in the conflagration of their own communities may be attempting to call the attention of a seemingly uncaring nation to their peril, made manifest when health inequities fueled by systemic racism make them more vulnerable to the coronavirus[6] and when some officers sworn to protect them seem intent on killing them. In effect, they are screaming to the world that they are not safe.

Yet, the paternalistic response by some officials has been to urge "good people" to stay home from protests, and others fret publicly that protests may lead to new coronavirus outbreaks.[7] Certainly, there is opportunity for virus transmission, but officials may miss the point that, among those whose existence is threatened on an ongoing basis, safety is relative.

Meanwhile, the need to enforce social distancing measures was cited as the rationale in Hong Kong for banning the annual June Fourth remembrance of those who died in the Tiananmen Square uprising.[8] Coming on the heels of China's security order reining in Hong Kong's autonomy, it seems apparent that the decision is more about protecting citizens there from democratic reform than from the virus.

The US, UK, Canada, and Australia issued a joint statement of condemnation against the new security law, but have so far stopped short of sanctions against China.[9] So, now the world waits for China's next move in Hong Kong, and the walls appear to be closing in on the democracy protesters there. The protesters have shown themselves to be nimble and resolute, so they may continue, but no one could legitimately argue that this security measure makes any of them safer.

Keeping citizens safe is a central governmental responsibility. In a public health emergency, this responsibility may entail infringing on essential liberties. If a government issues stay-at-home orders, it has the obligation of ensuring that people possess the fundamental securities needed to comply with the order. In many parts of the world, including the US, millions of people must work daily to survive. The pandemic only magnifies the stark reality of those who literally cannot afford to help keep their community safe by staying home, regardless of their intent.

Though originally blind to the needs and realities of its migrant workforce, Singapore quickly absorbed that lesson when migrant dormitories became epicenters for coronavirus outbreaks as conditions made it impossible for individuals to comply with isolation orders. The government responded by creating teams to supply them with food, medical care, Wi-Fi communication, and entertainment so that they could remain at home and actively help contain the virus.[10]

In the era of COVID-19, the phrase "stay safe" has become a mantra in some quarters—newscasters use it to sign off from broadcasts and some use the phrase to close emails to friends. But the phrase will remain hollow until we come to terms with who is safe in our society and who is not, even if it means acknowledging that some people in our midst are not safe from their own government.

23

The Children's Crusades

No, it wasn't just your imagination—political protests have become more widespread and frequent over the last several years. A Center for Strategic & International Studies report found that political protests increased worldwide by more than 11 percent annually from 2009 to 2019.[1] Such protests were reported across 114 countries in 2019 alone.

Pandemic stay-at-home orders and social distancing requirements had a chilling effect on large public protests, but the trend is expected to continue post-pandemic due to slow economic growth, the worsening impact of climate change, and disinformation tactics promoting agitation.

While university students are mainstays among protest crowds worldwide, younger participants have distinguished more recent political protests. Youth participation in social change movements is not a new phenomenon. The presence of African American children in many of the most notable 1960s civil rights demonstrations brought a particularly poignant focal point to public attention.[2] Now, many high school and middle school students have joined protest ranks on both sides of the Pacific and, in many instances, have played leadership roles.

The Thai democracy reform protests, which swelled to unprecedented public turnout levels in 2020, is a youth-led movement. Its hallmarks are heavily influenced by pop culture: The Hunger Games three-fingered salute as a sign of resistance, the protesters' use of giant, inflatable rubber duckies to shield themselves against water cannons fired by police.[3] This new generation of protesters' actions are characterized by quirky agitprop designed to provoke thought and engagement, rather than the heavy-handed symbolism of previous protest eras, such as the 2010 Red Shirt protests where blood was tossed at the home of Prime Minister Abhisit.[4] In contrast to historic characterization of protesters as angry, these protesters seem creative, lighthearted, and utterly unafraid—all of which makes them truly subversive.

At first glance, their leaders appear unlikely—they are nerdy and chubby, wear round glasses, and have nicknames like Penguin. They like to dress in Harry Potter costumes, sometimes even for court appearances, and would probably be the last chosen for a dodgeball team. They could be anyone's kids, and that is probably one of the reasons why they attracted such a large following from Bangkok's middle class to turn out for protests, drawing more than 10,000 participants in mid-2020.[5] That, and their demands are bolder: an end to harassment of legal expression and activism, the dissolution of parliament, a new constitution, and greater accountability of the monarchy under the constitution. Their approach may be lighthearted, but their intent is never less than serious.

While those demands were widely reported by Western media, another core demand made far fewer international headlines. Yet, this demand may be even more of a fundamental threat to the entrenched system of power that opposes democratic reforms in Thailand: reforming the harsh Thai primary and secondary education system.

"The stakeholders in the education system, the students, have long been oppressed. All Thai people know about the violent abuse in schools and have kept it under the rug for generations. But now, social media records and magnifies the abuses and makes it impossible to ignore," says Kunthida Rungruengkiat,[6] who was elected to the Thai Parliament as a member of the Future Forward Party prior to the party's forced dissolution in 2019. She is now banned for ten years from standing for public office along with other members of the party's executive committee. Public backlash to the abolition of the reformist Future Forward Party helped launch the current democratic protest movement.

Kunthida cites instances of "very weird corporal punishment" in schools, such as a student being forced to jump up and down repeatedly while balancing a heavy chair on his head and one student being forced to slap another student, as examples of a system designed to humiliate students. Though humiliation may be a tactic, she says that the system's goal is obedience. "The roots of the modern Thai education system come from the system to train civil servants, where the primary objective is obedience, to the king and the state," she says.

With the duty to obey inculcated in them from an early age, the Thai people's seeming resignation to the pendulum swings of periodic coups and the vicissitudes of its ever malleable constitution are perhaps more understandable. As an educator now who operates a bilingual primary school in Chiang Mai that stresses freedom of expression, Kunthida says the indoctrination is so strong that she sometimes encounters students who are literally afraid to take part in discussions about comparative systems of political hierarchy. But she says that more social media platforms and diverse news sources are helping students understand that it may be their right, or even their responsibility, to question authority in a democracy.

In the United States, the students at Marjory Stoneman Douglas High School in Parkland, Florida, helped galvanize public attention on the issue of gun control with their public protests following the Valentine's Day shooting at their school in 2018. Within days of the shooting, they had formed the organization Never Again MSD, which spearheaded school walkouts nationwide in support of gun control, culminating in a rally on the National Mall in Washington, DC, buttressed by parallel events in more than eight hundred cities worldwide.[7] One of the most salient impressions from that rally was of eighteen-year-old Emma Gonzalez, a Parkland shooting survivor, taking the speakers' podium to stand silently for six minutes and twenty seconds in recognition of the time it took for the school shooter to kill seventeen students and teachers, and wound another seventeen individuals.

Though momentum for gun control was at an all-time high in the immediate aftermath of the protests, comprehensive gun control has still not been enacted in the US. The Trump Administration's only legislative concession to school shooting protests was to pass the STOP School Violence Act, which entailed more money for metal detectors and training for security personnel.[8]

Right wing political commentators vilified the Parkland students as being manipulated by outside interests, and others attempting to undermine the validity of their accounts of the shooting and its aftermath labeled them "professional crisis actors."[9] Similarly, the young leaders of the Thai democracy movement have faced accusations of being controlled by *chung chart* or "nation-haters."[10] While it is true that the Parkland students accepted donations from outside groups to help build their organization, it is disingenuous to claim that the goals of either movement are not representative of the respective students.

Nuttaa Mahattana, a lecturer and media commentator with the nickname of "Bow" who has been a frequent speaker at Thai democracy rallies, said that the huge pro-democracy protests of August 2020 made her feel encouraged that the government might change.[11] By the time I spoke with her in March 2021, she said she had lost much hope for change in the near-term. She maintained that it is appropriate that the monarchy be included in demands for political reform even though Thai people are officially taught that the monarchy is above politics. "Each coup in the modern era was endorsed by the king at the time, so the monarchy is definitely political," she said. But she allows that including reform of the monarchy in current democratic demands may have been an overreach that has cost the movement crucial public support. "There has been a backlash from royalists, and this decision makes it easier for the older generation to claim that the students are being manipulated into protesting," she observed.

A mother to a ten-year-old son, Bow was recognized for publishing an online open letter to him explaining the motivations for the democracy protests.[12]

She also took him to observe the court proceedings against noted student activist Jatupat "Pai Dao Din" Boonpattararaksa. When asked about the proliferation of protesters at the high school and middle school levels, Bow said, "I am happy that they are thinking about their future and have become involved, but this also means that adults have failed to protect them and their right to a future."

With King Maha Vajiralongkorn's controversial moves to assume direct control of the Crown Property Bureau and two military units,[13] the monarchy may be at its modern apex of political power, rendering criticism of it a perilous undertaking. The government has increased prosecution under Section 112 of the constitution, the nation's strict lèse-majesté laws prohibiting insulting the monarchy. Several leaders of the current democracy movement have been jailed under lèse-majesté charges since February 2021, and many others are awaiting trial. This retaliatory atmosphere makes the students' ten-point declaration demanding reform of the monarchy on August 10, 2020 even more remarkable.[14]

In Thailand, the massive public protests of 2020 have morphed into the near deserted streets of 2021, and it is unclear whether this stems entirely from pandemic shutdown orders or whether the public is genuinely turning away from pursuing reform, though substantial pro-democracy chatter continues on social media. In the US, school shootings continue unabated, with multiple fatalities since the Parkland massacre.[15] Some critics might argue that both movements have failed, but it is difficult to evaluate political protest movements' capacity to affect long-term change, particularly if success is only measured by the broadest possible outcome—regime change in Thailand or comprehensive gun control in the US. Political accommodation and increased public discourse should also be viewed as valid markers of progress.

Facing the slim prospect of passing a federal comprehensive gun control law, the Never Again MSD students turned their attention to enacting policies at the state and local level. Since the Parkland shooting, new gun control measures have been enacted in twenty-six states.[16] Perhaps more significantly, the organization focused much of its education and outreach efforts on voter registration among students who were turning eighteen and newly eligible to vote. The 2020 elections marked an all-time high for participation of eighteen-year-old voters, a group with typically low turnout.[17]

Likewise, Kunthida points to what she says are lasting contributions to the cause of democracy in Thailand created in the brief two-year lifespan of the now dissolved Future Forward Party. "When we existed as a political party, we demanded that debate in parliament be broadcast. It was popular; people want to know what is going on. When we spoke in parliament, we used PowerPoint presentations with facts and figures that people could understand, not the overly formal rhetoric of our opponents," she says. The former lawmaker says that regardless of whether she or her Future Forward colleagues are in office, these innovations will remain because the culture of engagement has permanently changed.

"When we started, the impression of politicians was that they were all rich, dirty, and corrupt. We brought a new impression of politicians. Now, ordinary people can see themselves in politics," she says. Not even thirty-five years old when she was elected to parliament, Kunthida says she may run for office again after her ten-year ban from politics has ended.

The arc of any political or social change movement is long, marked by ebbs and flows along the way, with neither success nor failure being final, as the process is subject to continual evolution. Changes achieved today will be felt most profoundly in the future. It is only fitting that those destined to inherit the future have a role in shaping policies to address it, whether it is in the halls of parliament or on the streets.

24

Beyond Representation
Southeast Asian American
Political Participation

The final year of the Trump Administration, punctuated by a perfect storm of factors—pandemic scapegoating, a rise in anti-Asian violence, and Asian American political participation credited with helping win a national election—has created new visibility for the Asian American community. This visibility has resulted in more emphatic calls for representation, but there is disagreement as to what that means in this diverse community.

Though only comprising 6 percent of the US population, Asian Americans are the fastest growing racial group in the nation. Southeast Asian Americans account for approximately 14 percent of the broader Asian American community, and their history in the US is long, with the first community formed by seafaring Filipino "Manilamen" in Louisiana in the eighteenth century. The 1970s and 80s witnessed a wave of refugees to the US from Vietnam, Cambodia, and Laos, resulting from the protracted war in the region. In the twenty-first century, an influx of Karen refugees from Myanmar has helped further diversify the profile of Southeast Asian Americans.

While their histories and reasons for coming to the US are distinct, the narratives of Southeast Asian Americans have become entwined with those of Chinese Americans, Japanese Americans, and other Asian Americans. The twenty-first century expression of anti-Asian hate is painted with a broad brush and does not make distinctions based on ethnicity. Even though the Trumpian pandemic rhetoric that stoked this discrimination generally focused on China—

COVID-19 repeatedly called the "Chinese virus" and "kung flu"—one of the first instances of anti-Asian violence to capture widespread public attention was the fatal attack on Vicha Ratanapakdee, a Thai American octogenarian in California.[1]

In the state of Georgia, Asian Americans increased their voter turnout by 91 percent in the 2020 presidential election from the previous election in 2016.[2] Analysts tout this increase as helping deliver President Biden's only win in the Deep South and, perhaps even more importantly, cementing the Democratic edge in the US Senate, made complete by the tiebreaking vote of Vice President Kamala Harris, the first Asian American on a major party ticket. Though not yet seen as a political juggernaut, the community is gaining recognition for its potential and will certainly get more attention from future campaigns and candidates.

Such attention cannot come fast enough for Madalene Xuan-Trang Mielke, president of the Asian Pacific American Institute for Congressional Studies (APAICS), an organization with the mission of promoting Asian Pacific American participation and representation at all levels of the political process. "Campaigns do not actually see us. Most exit polls still lump us together as Other," she says.[3] Underlying the community's status as an untapped resource is the fact that most Asian American registered voters had not been contacted by either major party during the campaign cycle, the 2020 Asian American Voter Survey revealed.[4]

For the 2020 campaign cycle, APAICS prioritized outreach and education linking US Census participation with voter registration, sending the message that members of the community first must literally be counted to ensure that their views on policies are considered by elected officials. To candidates and campaigns hoping to harness the community's political energies, Mielke says, "Work to really understand our issues. Don't just assume we are part of your base vote."

The notion that the Asian American Pacific Islander (AAPI) community is not politically monolithic is also borne out through the 2020 Asian American Voter Survey, which indicated that Vietnamese American voters supported Trump over Biden, 48 to 36 percent respectively, and that they were also more likely to support Republican candidates in congressional races. The fact that most Vietnamese resettled in the US under the auspices of Republican administrations is generally thought to be a strong factor in their favorable view of the party.

Though the voter survey is the broadest instrument currently measuring Asian American positions, the only Southeast Asian American voters assessed by it are Filipino and Vietnamese Americans, and the only Southeast Asian language in which it is administered is Vietnamese. This begs the question as to whether Cambodians, Laotians, and Hmong who came to the US as a result of the Vietnam War have a similar affinity for the Republican Party. Clearly, more political analysis of these groups is needed.

Some Southeast Asian Americans who identified as Republican have left the party because of Trump's actions and rhetoric, most notably Charles Djou, a Thai American and the first Southeast Asian American elected to Congress in 2010. He released a public statement about his decision in 2018 that concluded, "But I am most disappointed by the failure of the GOP to clearly and consistently condemn Trump's childish behavior. Sadly today, too many Republicans either applaud Trump's tirades or greet them with silent acceptance. This leads to an implicit ratification by the GOP of Trump's undisciplined, uninformed, and unfocused leadership as a core part of the Republican Party."[5]

For Cambodians who experienced the horrors of the Killing Fields under the Khmer Rouge before resettling in the US, the prospect of political participation can be loaded with negative connotations. Their recollection of the genocide may link political participation with a one-way ticket to harassment, persecution, or death. Even decades of living in the US may not help overcome the association.

Darith Ung was born in Phnom Penh and spent years with his family fleeing the Khmer Rouge, first in Vietnam, then a Thai refugee camp, before immigrating to Canada as a teenager. He eventually wound up in Long Beach, California, with the largest concentration in the world of Cambodians outside Cambodia. When asked why so many Cambodians chose to settle there, he says it originally came down to one primary factor: the weather. Since refugees were allocated to communities in a geographically diverse manner to avoid overburdening any locality, many Cambodians first went to the chilly Northeast or frozen Quebec, as Ung did because of his father's French language skills. Ung says that the small group of Cambodians who landed in Long Beach began to lobby their compatriots about the warm weather and soon others began to move there. As they relocated, they built businesses within the community, which in turn became magnets for other Cambodians. "Now, we have insurance agencies, car repair shops, jewelry stores, grocery stores, all operated by Khmer speakers," he says.[6]

One of the most prevalent types of business in Long Beach's Cambodian network is the doughnut shop.[7] By some counts, there are as many as thirty in the area. Though not a traditional Cambodian delicacy, the community has taken to it by making standard American donuts alongside those flavored with pandan, coconut milk, and other Southeast Asian staples. One of the reasons the template worked for the first generation of Cambodian immigrants was that customers could simply point to their choice in the glass case, making English language fluency unnecessary.

Though older Cambodian immigrants may retain Khmer as a primary language, the push for assimilation frequently led subsequent generations to prioritize English, a theme common to the many diaspora stories around the world that have ended in the US. Ung is now a Khmer language instructor at California State University, Long Beach, a school known for its vibrant Khmer student community. He teaches Khmer to heritage speakers to help them reclaim their cultural ties to Cambodia and leads annual trips to Cambodia focusing on the country's history, which he says are primarily attended by non-Cambodian American students. He views both as important to strengthening the Cambodian community in the US and increasing understanding of it in broader American society.

Comfortable with traveling to Cambodia for visits, Ung has no desire to return to live there. Similarly, though he is a US citizen and voter, he avoids a visible role in politics, including turning out for rallies. "I am not an activist, just a teacher," he says.

For Southeast Asians who came to the US as children, their wartime memories may be less distinct and their immersion in American culture more encompassing, resulting in different views about political participation. Sandy Dang came from Vietnam to the US as a child, by way of a refugee camp in Hong Kong. After founding a leadership development program for Southeast Asian American youth in Washington, DC, she was chosen by the Obama Administration to direct its Vietnam Education Foundation, sponsoring Vietnamese science and technology students at US universities. Though she considers herself politically active, Dang's main passion remains education, and she views access to education as key to political participation within any community.

Like many Asian American activists, Dang stresses the importance of representation, whether within popular culture images or among elected officials, to reinforce members of the community's sense, particularly young people's sense, that they belong in American society. But is it enough to simply see an Asian face making decisions as an elected official or must that official also champion policies to help the Asian American community?

When pressed on the example of Elaine Chao, a prominent conservative whose business-first portfolio helped her become the first Asian American to serve in two presidential cabinets, Dang responded, "When electing or appointing someone, it is most important to me that they reflect my values. If they look like me, even better. But I don't think that [Chao] represents my values."[8]

Dang admits that she views her own identity as markedly Vietnamese American before being Asian American but says that it is more important than ever that Asian Americans unite to fight racism and anti-Asian hatred. Her sentiment highlights the dynamic tension at play between showing solidarity on prominent issues affecting the Asian American community while protecting distinct cultural and political interests from being subsumed.

The ongoing controversy over data disaggregation is a salient example of such tension. When writ large, the Asian American community compares favorably to other US demographic groups in terms of income and educational attainment, but when data is teased out by national origin, Southeast Asian Americans typically lag. Many advocates say that aggregating data disadvantages Southeast Asian Americans and leads to a lack of funding for programs and services that could help them bridge the gap.[9]

Case in point: the median income for Asian American Pacific Islander households in 2015 was $73,060, contrasted with $53,600 median income for all US households. But when broken down to reflect Southeast Asian American incomes, the advantage evaporates as annual median incomes for Hmong ($48,000), Burmese ($36,000), and Laotians ($15,000) were well under the overall median. Of the 2.5 million Southeast Asians who live in America, 1.1 million are considered low-income and approximately 460,000 live below the poverty line.

The economic divide is stark. A 2018 Pew Research Center report found that Asian Americans have the highest income inequality of any racial or ethnic group in the US and that Asian Americans in the top ten percent of income distribution earned 10.7 times as much as Asian Americans in the bottom ten percent.[10]

Disaggregated data also paints a revealing picture of educational attainment. Though more than half of Asian American adults hold a bachelor's degree, this aggregate measurement does not adequately represent Cambodian (18 percent), Hmong (17 percent), or Laotian (16 percent) college completion. Moreover, Southeast Asians have a high dropout rate, with 30 percent of Laotian and Vietnamese adults lacking a high school degree and 40 percent of Cambodian and Hmong adults having failed to complete high school.

Community advocates say that public reporting of aggregated data obscures the pressing needs of many Southeast Asian individuals and families. Policy at every level is increasingly driven by data, with grant distribution formulae shaped by a variety of statistical instruments. Many Southeast Asian community development proponents assert that disaggregating data by national origin will result in more effectively tailored anti-poverty and dropout prevention programs to uplift those with the greatest needs.

Not all Asian Americans are as sanguine about the benefits of data disaggregation. Recent immigrants from mainland China have led strong pushback.[11] Frequently, affirmative action is the driving issue of dissent, with many recent Chinese immigrants voicing fears that disaggregated data will be used to show overrepresentation of some Asian groups at leading US universities, which might prevent their children from gaining admission to Ivy League schools.

Five US states have passed legislation requiring public agencies to collect more detailed information about Asian Americans in their communities broken down by ethnicity. The Obama Administration began implementing data disaggregation efforts through the White House Initiative on Asian Americans and Pacific Islanders, but the Trump Administration's dumpster fire census work left unclear whether that work was being replicated. The delayed detailed demographic results of the 2020 Census may paint a clearer picture.

While the census can help develop a narrative of Southeast Asian Americans in statistical form, others use more traditional storytelling to underscore the experiences of their community. "The term 'American' can be fraught for

Southeast Asians. A lot depends on how you got here," says Chinada Phaengdara Potter, executive director of the Southeast Asian Diaspora (SEAD) Project, a Minneapolis-based initiative that seeks to build social empowerment through cultural organizing. She says the Hmong, Vietnamese, Cambodian, Laotian, and Burmese people she works with "hold many histories."[12]

Potter came to the US with her family from Laos when she was three years old. After living for decades in the US, her father moved back to Laos upon his retirement. (Similarly, Ung's father and older brother returned to live in Cambodia after they retired from jobs in Canada). "Many of our elders yearn to go back," she says.

But the return is not always smooth. Upon his arrival, officials interrogated Potter's father for hours to ensure that he posed no threat to the government before being allowed to return to his village. Because Laos does not recognize dual citizenship, he will not be able to inherit property his parents had wanted him to have, but she says he is still content with life on the family farm.

Potter agrees that later generation Southeast Asian immigrants are more likely to be politicized than their parents. "When our elders first arrived here, they were in survival mode, so they had no time or interest for politics," she says. She points to extensive intergenerational work done through many community organizations to help second and third generation Southeast Asian Americans reach out to involve first generation immigrants in census participation and voting in the 2020 elections.

The SEAD Project benefits from a plethora of rich cultural materials provided by the Hmong community in Minneapolis and St. Paul, where the largest urban concentration of Hmong in the US live, including Olympic gold medal gymnast Suni Lee. There are more than 82,000 Hmong in the metropolitan area, and they are working to integrate themselves into the state's political fabric, with five recently elected to the Minnesota state legislature.

The story of Hmong in the Twin Cities also reflects the complicated and nuanced confluence of Asian American and African American race relations in the US. While many young Hmong activists are working as active allies in the Black Lives Matter movement, it is also true that one of the police officers who prevented bystanders from intervening in George Floyd's murder on May 25, 2020 and who was subsequently charged with aiding and abetting Floyd's murder is Hmong American.[13] Like most things about the Southeast Asian American community, it defies facile generalization.

This diversity of political views has led some progressive AAPI activists to borrow a phrase from other minority activists: Not all skinfolk are kinfolk. "I empathize with people trying to find a political home," says Potter. "But it has been difficult for me to see Trump supporters in our community because of the harm he has done to us. It was hard to see some of our own people excusing the deportation of members of our community."

She agrees with Dang that representation must go beyond face value. "Representation is important, but if it's not rooted in equity, then the system will still nurture injustice," she says. She says that the further people are from their own heritage and histories, the more likely they are to embrace principles that bolster an unjust society. The SEAD Project works to help the Southeast Asian immigrant community, through storytelling, art, and language skills, reclaim collective values they may have jettisoned in the initial struggle for survival upon arrival.

Parallel to political visibility, representation in popular culture is subject to intense social media criticism. The animated film *Raya and the Last Dragon* grabbed both laudatory and accusatory headlines.[14] The film was celebrated for introducing the first Southeast Asian Disney princess, but was criticized for fabricating the Southeast Asian kingdom of Kumandra as its setting, showing its customs as an amalgam of the cultures of several countries in the region.

Potter is enthusiastic about what the cartoon character represents for her eight-year-old daughter: "When I first came to this country, I tried hard to find faces that looked like mine, but I didn't see many. I am glad that she can see a face that looks like hers in that movie." She allows that it is problematic that the film synthesized distinct cultures into one, but says it is important that the studio used a Southeast Asian story trust to borrow authentically from various heritages.

Amidst all the energy and excitement of the nascent political participation of Southeast Asian Americans, there is still a palpable sense of pain and loss when talking with many first-generation immigrants. Julie Diep, who arrived in California from central Vietnam as a young child with her family in the late 1970s, is using her own need for healing to help her community.

Her given name is Bang Chau, which she says means "snow white gem" in Vietnamese, but was given the name Julie after arriving in the US. "We tried so hard to assimilate that we let go of a lot along the way," she says.[15]

Diep says she was taught by her mother to always be respectful, so she never fought back, even when bullied. Her older brothers took on the fights for everyone in their family, and their adjustment to American life was rocky. This is part of what fuels Diep's sadness, as one brother spent years in prison and the other died due to substance abuse.

She first returned to Vietnam at the age of twenty-three and was unprepared for the culture shock. She says she became ill from food and was repulsed by what she saw as filth there. Though she was supposed to stay in the country for two weeks, she went to a travel agency after a couple of days to change her return ticket so that she could depart immediately. It has only been in the last few years that she has returned to Hue and reconnected with a culture she now sees as her own.

Despite struggling with learning disabilities and depression, Diep became a speech pathologist and founded an organization dedicated to increasing understanding and awareness of autism in the Asian American community. As a community advocate, she was encouraged by others to run for office.

Her status as a small business proprietor and gun owner originally led to an affinity with the Republican Party. But while in Hue in 2019, she spent time pondering the need for services in her community and decided that Democratic-promoted policies would be more effective, so she registered as a Democratic candidate for the city council of Garden Grove, California. Narrowly defeated in the 2020 election, Diep says that she may run again but is concentrating now on raising funds to build a local Vietnamese American community center that will incorporate both Buddhist and Christian principles to emphasize compassion and healing.

Born in Bangkok to a Thai mother and an American GI father, Tammy Duckworth grew up in Thailand, Cambodia, Indonesia, and Singapore before settling in Hawaii with her family as a teenager, where her father's chronic unemployment led her to take on the role of breadwinner by selling roses on the side of the highway for a few dollars a day. After her itinerant childhood spent moving around Southeast Asia, it is somewhat surprising that she found a home in rural Illinois, the first impression of which she describes in her memoir as "weirdly comforting, like a place I knew in my bones."[16]

She now represents Illinois in the US Senate and is the first Southeast Asian American elected to the Senate. Her role in politics began after a distinguished career as an Army helicopter pilot. She was shot down in Iraq and lost both legs. Her story is punctuated by elements of economic deprivation, racial discrimination, and intergenerational conflict, but comes across, in her telling, as more of a twenty-first century Horatio Alger story in which the plucky heroine finally makes it to the top, with plenty of character-building challenges along the way. Rather than sadness or grief, the emotion that she most publicly expresses is gratitude—from the subsidized school meals that helped feed her when she first arrived in Hawaii to the US military that gave her the opportunity to fulfill her ambition as a pilot.

Along the way, Duckworth became a savvy politician who learned to take advantage of public optics to make her move. AAPI leaders voiced profound disappointment for months that President Biden had not appointed any Asian Americans as cabinet secretaries (he had appointed Katherine Tai as US Trade Representative, which is not generally recognized as part of the cabinet). However, the mass shooting of Asian American women working at two Atlanta massage parlors on March 16, 2021 and the subsequent public outrage created a new level of focus on the community and opened a narrow window for action.

Duckworth joined with Mazie Hirono, the only other Asian American currently serving in the US Senate, and threatened to block any further non-minority presidential nominees in protest over the lack of AAPI representation in the cabinet.[17] With a current partisan tie in the senate, the loss of two votes could doom future nominees. Biden immediately responded by committing to add a senior level AAPI liaison and to restart the White House Initiative on Asian Americans and Pacific Islanders with an initial focus on anti-Asian bias and violence.[23]

The stories of Southeast Asian Americans continue to write themselves across the United States, from doughnut shops in Southern California to the halls of Congress. When asked what he wishes Americans knew about Cambodians, Darith Ung says, "We are smart people. Some people only think that maybe Japanese and Chinese are smart, but we are smart, too, and we want to succeed. We are just a little bit under the radar."[18]

Under the radar. The same could be said of the broader Southeast Asian American community. It will be incumbent on electoral candidates to do the work to understand the communities' take on issues, which will necessitate a better grasp on history, language, and culture. Concerns about under-sampling should not scare campaigns away from including Southeast Asian Americans in polls. Further, campaigns should work with heritage speakers to develop literature, rather than rely on Google Translate.

Above all, policymakers should avoid assumptions about the type of initiatives that Southeast Asian Americans will support, even those affecting the ASEAN region. It should not be taken for granted that all Southeast Asian Americans want to see Chinese influence in the region curtailed or that there is widespread support for sanctions against the military junta in Myanmar if there is a perception that the policy will carry deep collateral damage for ordinary citizens there. Likewise, the issue of immigration cuts both ways with some calling for comprehensive reform on the forced repatriation of Southeast Asians, while others in the community worry that easing restrictions on who can enter the US will invite those who do not want to work hard.

It is sometimes possible to pinpoint a critical moment in various American civil rights movements that galvanized the community and led to a higher level of cohesion and action. For the gay rights movement, the Stonewall riots provided that moment. For the deaf culture movement, it occurred when Gallaudet University enraged its alumni by summarily rejecting calls for a deaf president.

In both instances, there was already a long tradition of community organizing against injustices, but these occurrences served as tipping points in which activists assumed the mantle of a movement and the public began to acknowledge its collective power. The March 16, 2021 killing of six Asian women who worked at Atlanta massage parlors, callously explained by a law enforcement official as being conducted by a man who was "having a bad day," is being recognized by some as such a moment for the AAPI community.

Some AAPI activists, however, caution against haste in explaining the moment and crafting immediate policy responses. Many of those I spoke with talked about the need to grieve and for healing as being the most pressing concerns for their community. They seek the space to do this.

While this respect for stillness and spiritual contemplation necessary for healing honors traditional Southeast Asian roots, it may be at odds with mainstream political activism in the US, which, inspired by Dr. Martin Luther King Jr.'s entreaty about "the fierce urgency of now," seeks to capitalize on such singular moments to achieve progress. Activists within the community will ultimately decide the pace of movement and whether there is room for those who aren't ready to march forward in lock step.

Whatever the reverberations of these extraordinary times within the community, policymakers and politicians who ignore the growing group of Southeast Asian American voters do so at their own peril. The Year 2020, a year like no other, may have finally awakened the sleeping tiger of AAPI political participation, and it won't be going back to sleep any time soon.

25

What Lies Ahead

During his turbulent tenure, President Trump's engagement with Southeast Asia seemed superficial at best. Besides his initial participation in the 2017 Asia Pacific Economic Cooperation Summit, his only other visit to the region was to use it as a neutral setting for meeting with North Korea's Kim Jong-un.[1]

Sorting through the Trump Administration's hyperbolic rhetoric, disjointed action, and musical chairs personnel lineup to identify a consistent foreign policy regarding Southeast Asia proved daunting. Retreat from multilateralism and weakened support for institutions supporting it emerged as two of the few consistent themes.

Within months of his election, Trump had initiated withdrawal from the Paris Agreement, the Trans-Pacific Partnership Agreement, the Iran nuclear deal, and the United Nations Education, Scientific and Cultural Organization (UNESCO).[2] As the coronavirus pandemic laid siege around the world, Trump gave the UN formal notification of intent to withdraw from the World Health Organization.[3] These were all clear signals of the US aim to abdicate responsibility for helping craft solutions to the world's most pressing problems.

Certainly, there were devastating issues gripping the US in the past four years that called for focused leadership—the effects of climate change, growing economic inequality, legacies of racial injustice, and the coronavirus pandemic. But these same problems were being experienced around the world. Such massive, complex problems require the resources and commitments of many thinkers, policymakers, and nations to effectively address.

But even if Trump had a consistent thematic policy toward Southeast Asia, there would have been few actors to help him implement it. By the forty-fifth president's first anniversary in office, 34 percent of his senior staff had quit or been forced out.[4] This rate is in sharp contrast to the two immediate past administrations, in which Obama experienced a 9 percent turnover and George W. Bush experienced a 6 percent turnover in their first year in office. These staffing deficiencies were even more profoundly felt in the absences in key diplomatic roles. Trump left vacant the seat of Assistant Secretary for East Asia at the Department of State as well as the ambassadorships to Australia and Singapore for almost the entire term of his presidency.

Once-valued partners might have wondered if their relationship with the US still mattered to this president. This seeming disregard for Southeast Asia was coincident with fashionable embrace of the term "Indo-Pacific" within geopolitical security circles that had begun before his administration. I confess a particular aversion to the term and the frequently mentioned imperative to maintain a free and open Indo-Pacific. It suggests strategic navigation channels, be they maritime or broadband, maintained by the elite Quad powers (US, Australia, Japan, and India) without acknowledging the agency of the billions of people who live within those dimensions in Asia. *No one lives in the Indo-Pacific.*

With its arrival in 2021, the Biden Administration announced a commitment to diplomacy that had all but disappeared during the last four years. Southeast Asian leaders will look for commitments to the president's participation in the Asia Pacific Economic Cooperation and the East Asia Summits. They have also been busy combing through details from the new administration's early days to gauge its intentions.

White House phone logs indicate that Biden, like Trump, did not hold phone discussions or meetings with any Southeast Asian leaders during his first hundred days in office.[5] Perhaps unsurprisingly, he convened a virtual summit of Quad leaders during those early days, indicating the strategic value he places on that alliance. They are powerful nations and trusted allies, and the importance of maintaining strong relationships with them is clear, but it would be a mistake to send the region a message, however subtle, that these Fab Four intend to police the area with a sense of entitlement. Southeast Asian nations will scrutinize any overtures from the US for indication of whether the new administration views them as worthy of mature partnership or as mere markers on the Indo-Pacific game board.

In June of 2021, Deputy Secretary of State Wendy Sherman completed the Biden Administration's first high-level trip to Southeast Asia, visiting Cambodia, Thailand, and Indonesia.[6] Those countries represent three distinct profiles illustrating where Southeast Asian nations may fall on a spectrum of US influence and underscore the critical importance of establishing an independent relationship with each nation separate from any regional posture. Cambodia represents the most ideologically and pragmatically distant reach, as its already close relationship with China has grown even tighter over the past four years, culminating in US sponsored naval facilities being razed and supplanted by new

Chinese built structures.[7] Chinese military encroachment in the region will be an active concern for the new administration, but since the relationship with Cambodia has historically been remote, the recent moves cannot be considered a complete reversal. The Biden Administration is likely more concerned by what may be interpreted as a shift away from the US orbit by Thailand, traditionally seen as a strong regional ally. Though the Obama Administration criticized the most recent Thai coup, joint military exercises continued and Thailand was placed in an improved position on the US State Department's Trafficking in Persons Report. But Prime Minister Prayut's close relationship with the junta in Myanmar remains a cause of concern for the US and other partners in the region.[8] Indonesia, a strong advocate for the Assocation of Southeast Asian Nations taking a more robust stance regarding the junta in Myanmar, was upheld by Sherman during the trip as "an anchor of the rules-based order in the Indo-Pacific."[9] It is of note that, unlike Indonesia, Thailand shares a border with Myanmar and China comes within a hundred kilometers of its territory, underscoring the key political tenet that where you sit determines where you stand. This does not mean that Thailand's siding with China or Myanmar would be automatic, merely that sharing a land border makes their considerations about such issues as cross-border migration or territorial disputes different than Indonesia's.

Even if the Biden Administration makes energetic strides to reestablish stronger diplomatic relations in the region, the road ahead may not be smooth because significant ground has been lost over the past four years. The 2020 State of Southeast Asia Survey, an annual poll of key regional policymakers, academics, and influencers conducted by the National University of Singapore's Institute of Southeast Asian Studies (ISEAS), found that more than 80 percent of respondents thought that US engagement within the region had diminished during the Trump Administration.[10]

This should surprise no one. We cannot all but disappear from constructive diplomacy within a region for years and assume that its nations will stand still awaiting our return. Nature abhors a vacuum and so do strategic alliances. The 2020 survey also found that the European Union has eclipsed the US as Southeast Asia's most trusted partner regarding the rule of law.[11] It would be damaging for the US to be seen on its reengagement with the region as lecturing on human rights, but Biden's key diplomatic players know that it will be necessary to win back trust by continuing to urge other nations' commitment and progress on the rule of law, transparency, and human rights, while acknowledging instances where the US has fallen short in its record.

Other survey findings illuminate potential cases for the US to use soft power. Despite an overall diminished view of America, respondents still pointed to the US as the most desired destination for an international scholarship, barely edging out the UK. It makes sense to capitalize on this narrow advantage and continue to strengthen people-to-people exchanges with Southeast Asian students, scholars, and emerging professionals through international education programs.

But there is ample room for growth in other soft power arenas. Only 5 percent of respondents reported that they had high regard for US culture. As a reflection of the steady diet of Stallone and Kardashians that the region has been fed for decades, this is not surprising and highlights gains to be made if the US took a more organized and proactive approach to its cultural identity abroad. South Korea's strategic decision to make its cultural exports a primary trading commodity has paid off in droves, not just economically, but in a more positive global image. Even if a US focus on exporting quality cultural products only resulted in incremental gains in attitudes in the region, the overall trend would be helpful, as there is virtually nowhere to go but up at present.

There is much work to be done in establishing the US as a worthy international partner, not just because of increased global skepticism of American capacity and commitment, but also because of the fractured American populace. In the beginning of 2021, individuals who sought to overturn the legitimate results of a national election led a violent assault on the US Capitol. It is a grim irony that the day was January 6, the Christian holiday of Epiphany. The events of that day served as a revelation of sorts, bringing clarity to the fact that though the Trump presidency was ending, the effects of the Trump Era will be with us for a long time to come.

Beyond the vile and savage actions of that day, the true epiphany it represents has far more pervasive meaning. Despite the media emphasis and public fixation during the past four years on all things Trump—his language, his arrogance, his ignorance, and his appearance—it was never really about him. It was about us all along.

Americans are capable of greatness, in thought, action, and spirit, but we are also capable of mounting an insurrection because we do not agree with the results of a lawful election. The epiphany continues: In 2016, many Trump supporters, fearing ridicule, kept their leanings private, likely contributing to the skewed opinion polls which predicted a Hillary Clinton victory. But in 2021, those who ascribe to what is now known as Trumpism no longer feel the need to hide. They are our neighbors and coworkers and decision makers in some of the highest offices in the land. It was not a temporary fever dream from which we are waking. This is America. It is time to sit with the dissonance.

But the events of the past four years have also served as a rebuke to those who would take us down an isolationist path, locking arms and chanting America First, because there are far more Americans now who understand that our most pressing challenges are simply too complex to be shouldered alone. And there is a growing realization that the US economy is too globally interconnected to think that remedies crafted to benefit us alone will not create negative effects for other nations that come back to us eventually.

Mundane issues, like the supply chain, which had not previously occupied public attention have moved to the forefront of thoughtful debate, as Americans who had never known scarcity had brushes with temporary deprivation during the pandemic. Who knew pre-COVID that most of the world's latex surgical gloves were produced in Malaysia?[12] The fallout from supply chain disruptions argues that we must strengthen American manufacturing while simultaneously paying more attention to labor conditions in Southeast Asia.

Biden laid out the initial thinking for this undertaking in his Interim National-al Security Strategic Guidance, issued in March of 2021. Without explicit reference to Trump, the document acknowledges that the past four years have weakened the US's capacity and image abroad. It also makes clear Biden's belief that "America's fate is inextricably linked to events beyond our shores." The treatise prioritizes engagement with Southeast Asia, as it articulates, "Our vital national interests compel the deepest connection to the Indo-Pacific." It even orders the region's importance before Europe and the Western Hemisphere. Further, it commits the US to "deepen our partnership with . . . Singapore, Vietnam, and other ASEAN member states, to advance shared objectives."[13]

Biden's strategic guidance does not enumerate the shared objectives it envisions in the region, but it acknowledges that "the distribution of power across the world is changing" and identifies China as a potential threat. It is not much of a leap in reasoning to think that countering China is one such "shared objective" the Biden Administration has in mind for Southeast Asian nations. But it would be unfortunate if that objective were to characterize engagement efforts in the region. Clearly, the US will continue working to check China's quest for global influence, but if that comes to dominate relations with Southeast Asian nations, it will be impossible to create or maintain the trusting partnerships to which the administration claims it aspires.

US efforts regarding the Mekong River are a prime example. More than sixty million people currently rely on the Mekong Delta for their livelihood, but the effects of climate change and energy demands spurred by population growth and increased industrialization jeopardize their subsistence as well as the region's unique ecosystem.

Attempts to harness the river's resources for individual nations' exploitation without regional coordination have created the type of trans-boundary challenge that cries out for the subtle assistance of diplomatic good offices. Annual fish haul in Cambodia's Tonlé Sap has decreased dramatically in recent years; explosive Laotian investment in hydropower has modified water flow and endangered downstream wildlife; climate change has degraded cultural heritage monuments in the region, including Vietnam's fabled lotus fields; and traditional rice farming techniques fail to meet the demand of feeding a growing population and thwart sustainable land use goals.[14, 15, 16, 17] These are all areas where US technical expertise and investment can go a long way to help rebuild ties in the region.

In September 2020, the Trump Administration announced a new Mekong-US Partnership with the Lower Mekong nations—Cambodia, Laos, Myanmar, Thailand, and Vietnam—for critical research and development projects on disaster management, environmental sustainability, and cross-border crime.[18] The Mekong's flow into the South China Sea carries enormous strategic implications, and the nascent Biden Administration will likely work to strengthen Quad involvement in the region.

But further strategic efforts regarding the Mekong will be ineffective without the involvement of China. The river originates in the Tibetan plateau of China and is shared by the five Lower Mekong nations. Yet, China's construction of dams along the Mekong (called the Lancang in China) has been blamed for historic downriver flooding in previous decades and has more recently been linked to devastating droughts in 2019 and 2020. The new US-Mekong Partnership helped fund the Mekong Dam Monitor, an online platform that is housed at a nongovernmental organization. The NGO is linked with a report that criticized China's "impounding" the river's water to deny it from the lower basin nations.[19] At a March 2021 Stimson Center plenary on the US-Mekong Partnership Track Policy Dialogue that focused on lower basin cooperation, Brian Eyler, the center's Southeast Asian program director, commented, "The [People's Republic of China] is not responding to downriver concerns."[20]

The proliferation of Chinese dams has created negative environmental consequences for the lower basin, but it is disingenuous to suggest that China has been entirely unresponsive to downriver issues. Almost a decade ago, China formed the Lancang-Mekong Cooperation to engage in regional water management and development projects.[21] In 2020, China began sharing hydrological data with downriver nations to help effectively manage water flow and ameliorate the effects of diversion, but this came only after significant pressure from the US and other allied nations.

It will be necessary to cut through propaganda on both sides to get an accurate picture of issues affecting the Mekong region. To the extent that China is part of the problem, it must also be part of the solution, but this will not happen if it is not invited to the table on consultative projects. It is equally important to admit the role that hydropower has, and will have, on lessening the region's dependence on coal, a strong global positive, and to focus more intently on managing consequences, rather than continue to attempt to use the issue as an ideological wedge. Options possible for US involvement with China in Southeast Asia include cooperation, competition, and conflict. Scenarios involving each of those options are easily envisioned. For the sake of the region, hopefully cooperation will prevail on the Mekong.

Similarly, the US must expect and invite China's participation in developing constructive solutions to the crisis in Myanmar. The history of Burma's emergence from postcolonial era to tentative steps toward democracy was far more complex than the simplistic good versus evil fable many in the US still believe.[22] Difficult as it may be to accept given their brutal crackdown on pro-democracy protesters, the ruling cadre of generals is not likely to go away any time soon. But the junta clearly misjudged the depth of opposition, particularly among young people who have come of age in an era not characterized by the isolation of previous generations. During my visits to the country over the past twenty years, I have borne witness to enormous change and the people's growing connection with the outside world that will make it virtually impossible for the younger generation to resign itself to living under the junta.

The Biden Administration can be confident that the American people deplore the junta's violent backlash against protesters, but it should be equally clear there is scant public appetite for intervention beyond sanctions, making it even more important that the US welcome China as a key actor in helping reach resolution in Myanmar. Trans-boundary considerations lend a clear emphasis to China's participation. If for no other reason than avoiding massive default on Belt and Road Initiative project debt if Myanmar becomes a failed state, China may be willing to help broker a way forward.

The shifting balance of global power may necessitate creation of new alliances outside the traditional superpower narrative, yet most news coverage and commentary signal the tired trope that Southeast Asian nations have no resort but to align themselves with either the US or China. We should expect that, as sovereign nations, they each have their own independent relationships with the US and with China. These relationships will play out differently depending on the issue. Chinese vaccine diplomacy efforts were described by Laotian President Bounnhang Vorachit as exemplifying a "comradely relationship of cooperation" that "demonstrates the spirit of Laos-China community with a shared future," while similar Chinese pandemic outreach was viewed more skeptically in Vietnam.[23] Other examples abound: Myanmar has allowed a growing share of its GDP to be subsumed by debt through Belt and Road Initiative infrastructure projects, while Malaysia, led by a new president who rejected saddling future generations with debt, successfully renegotiated the terms of agreement for their Belt and Road Initiative development projects with China.[24] And the Philippines's Duterte frequently employs the aphorism, "when elephants fight, the grass gets trampled," to justify steering clear of taking sides in any US/China decision, relishing in his nonaligned posture by handing out public tongue-lashings to both countries, which do nothing to erode the historically strong ties between the US and the Philippines.[25]

Not only do we fall short when we expect other nations to conform to this either/or construct, but we also use it to our disadvantage at home. The rhetoric used to describe US foreign policy initiatives is too often reduced to a simplistic dichotomy expressing support for America remaining strong at home or serving as the world's policeman. Such a framework is an outmoded attempt to force contemporary foreign policy decisions into neat categories that fails to recognize the myriad ways globalization has fostered interdependence among nations, requiring a nuanced, collective approach both comprehensive and nimble enough to address twenty-first century challenges. The scourges of climate change, economic inequality, and the rapidly transforming use of social media disinformation to undermine democracies are not confined within the borders of any one nation. Nor can their resolutions be.

This is the Herculean task before Secretary of State Antony Blinken as he attempts to implement the Biden imperative linking foreign and domestic policy in a way in which progress in one sphere is not made at the expense of the other. The thinkers behind the administration's new doctrine have come up with a few catchy names for it—"A Foreign Policy for the Middle Class" and "A Foreign Policy that Works for American Workers."[26] While bumper sticker slogans are part of any campaign, the test of the doctrine will be the American reaction to some of its earliest objectives.

As devastating as the pandemic has been, it has also delivered the opportunity of vaccine diplomacy to demonstrate to the world that the US is ready for constructive reengagement and to reinforce to the American public that we cannot be strong at home without also being strong abroad. The Trump Administration was criticized for refusing to join the COVAX effort to supply vaccines to economically under-resourced nations, but Biden also came into the line of fire for initially focusing on buying more vaccine doses for the US. Then, as some US states began to reach the 70 percent threshold of vaccination, Biden made a bold announcement in support of the TRIPS waiver regarding intellectual property in pharmaceutical patents, which will make it easier for other nations to manufacture and distribute coronavirus vaccines.[27]

The timing of the announcement demonstrates the pragmatic knife-edge that the administration needs to walk to implement its promoted linkage of foreign and domestic priorities. Biden faced pressure from day one, from both within and without his administration, to demonstrate the compassion that international observers found lacking over the last four years and show that the US was ready to again resume global engagement. But American vaccination efforts were foundering, COVID-19 fatality rates were climbing toward the half million mark, and an attempt to prioritize vaccine access in other parts of the world would have been savaged in the US, likely even by Biden supporters. Embodying the airline safety mantra to secure your own mask in the event of an emergency before helping others, Biden made a full court press for US vaccination before pivoting in a manner forceful enough to draw the ire of the powerful pharmaceutical lobby with his support for the TRIPS waiver. The appointment of former UN Ambassador Samantha Power to head the US Agency for International Development underscores the administration's commitment to using humanitarian aid to bolster strategic relationships.[28]

In Secretary Blinken's first major speech in March 2021, outlining how his team plans to help implement Biden's interim strategic guidance, he admitted that individuals helming US diplomacy need to do a better job of "connecting it to the needs and aspirations of the American people."[29] He gave weight to the lofty complementarity of actions around the world that will "make us stronger here at home" as well as domestic actions that will make us "stronger in the world." It is a tall order to be sure, but a necessary approach to win support from an American public that has grown increasingly wary of international engagement at a time when domestic problems go unanswered.

In that first policy speech, Blinken also made the commitment to "work with Congress whenever we can." This carries the implication that there will be times when the new administration is prepared to act without congressional support. It is the responsibility of the US Senate to ratify treaties, but only a small fraction of American diplomatic efforts wind up memorialized in treaties, so it remains ambiguous as to where congressional approval will be sought. Such an approval process would likely be slow and characterized by incremental steps, as the current US Senate is clearly divided on a partisan basis, with stalwart Republicans still casting long shadows and recalcitrant Democrats standing in the way of home runs from the new administration. Blinken's tip of the hat to Congress is more than feel-good, inclusive rhetoric, but an acknowledgement of the pervasive polarization of the American public and tacit admission that taking foreign policy positions that are not supported by the public will likely make Biden a one-term president.

Leaders of Southeast Asian nations are right to view initial American diplomatic efforts with both cautious optimism and healthy skepticism, knowing as they do that Biden's mandate to return the US to global engagement is slim and could easily be reversed in the next election. Does acknowledging that US foreign policy is subject to the vicissitudes of electoral politics mean that there are no fundamentally enduring American principles that can be asserted on the world stage? And does seeking public buy-in for foreign policy actions make it more likely that those actions will reflect consistent principles or the mutability of political opinion?

Fortunately, there is exciting intergovernmental international engagement outside the political stalemate that constrains Congress and Foggy Bottom, where the US State Department resides.[30] Indeed, much of the most productive international policy collaboration currently occurs between cities on a range of practical considerations with far-reaching implications, from new technology for water data collection to ways to leverage the Olympic games to support women-owned businesses. Collaboration at the subnational level tends to focus on pragmatic problem-solving and skirts ideology. As more linkages are established, engagement will be more firmly ingrained, helping to insulate policies from partisan pendulum swings.

Democracies are volatile, and election results can be unpredictable. Like the 2016 US election, the most recent national elections in Malaysia and Australia resulted in surprise outcomes. The 2018 Malaysian election resulted in the first regime change in the country's history, as the Pakatan Harapan coalition ousted the Barisan Nasional Party, which had held power since the nation's independence in 1957.[31] Similarly, the 2019 Australian election resulted in an upset victory for the incumbent Liberal Party, as polls had consistently shown the opposition Labor leading throughout the campaign.[32]

In the case of electoral surprises, the postmortem generally focuses on the losing side's attempts to diagnose how and where polling failed, masking an absolute refusal to believe that their fellow citizens could have made a political choice diametrically opposed to their own. But, as Shakespeare reminds us, the fault is not in our stars, but in ourselves. That simple realization is absent from much of the current analysis around political polarization in the US. It is easier to wrap our heads around technological culprits than to grapple with the puzzle of how humans in our midst can see things so differently than we do.

Many leaders in the US have hit fast-forward and are making pronouncements about healing the divide in what has become a political chasm before fully understanding the cause of the schism. Certainly, we must strive for greater harmony, particularly if we want to address big challenges as a nation, but it may benefit us to first acknowledge, and sit with, the dissonance for a while. Sitting with discomfort or dissonance is part of the process of contemplation, which may ultimately allow us to articulate a shared vision of America not built on platitudes but on words and deeds more representative of all its citizens, to which we will hold ourselves accountable.

What type of policy framework then would allow us to acknowledge dissonance without diminishing the primacy of key principles or objectives? Perhaps, a model could be found in ASEAN. Frequently dismissed in the West as an ineffective regional power broker, the organization's operation may still provide lessons about how to ride out these turbulent times. Though its founding principles of consensus and nonintervention generally receive the most notice and criticism from US observers, the organization's historical emphasis on conflict reduction, rather than conflict resolution, merits more attention.[33] Man-made circumstances, including widening economic inequality and aggressive political disinformation campaigns, make this era increasingly volatile. It could make sense to adopt ASEAN's more subtle approach at times, conserving strategic resources by focusing on conflict reduction or management, rather than expending more resources in the higher-risk goal of conflict resolution. Such a focus could allow more resources to go to the amelioration and elimination of underlying causes of conflict to achieve greater harmony over time.

The Biden Administration has signaled intent to return to multilateral engagement, certainly on big-ticket issues, though this may not happen in the near-term in every instance. In the meantime, there will be a range of opportunities for bilateral participation with Southeast Asian nations on a range of discreet issues, in part to demonstrate US commitment to being viewed again as a trusted ally in the region.

Traditionally, members of the US foreign policy establishment have shared similar backgrounds as primarily white males from upper income families and elite schools. The dearth of community role models made aspiration to foreign service careers a rarity for people of color and those from working class backgrounds. Biden made a symbolically significant declaration of his intent to remake this narrow image of diplomatic professionals by naming Linda Thomas-Greenfield, an African American woman with degrees from public state universities who worked her way up through the ranks over a thirty-year foreign service career, as his UN Ambassador.[34]

Honing presidential rhetoric to link foreign policy decisions to domestic challenges can help build support for US involvement in global initiatives, but exposing more low- and middle-income Americans to international experiences and perspectives could be even more useful. International travel can help create a broader worldview, but such travel can be cost-prohibitive for working class people. Many students get their first immersive exposure to international cultures through study abroad programs, but the soaring cost of higher education is forcing fewer children from working class families to enroll in college. Also, predictions about the radically changed future of work have many young people questioning the value of a college degree.

Creating new initiatives to provide low- and middle-income Americans with international exposure will help ensure that there is a voting majority supportive of US global engagement. For young people not attending college, the creation of apprentice programs that include in-residence international cross-training could be useful. Expanding the number and type of Peace Corps jobs as well as creating other public programs to promote international volunteerism for working Americans of all ages without college degrees could help more US citizens realize the link between foreign and domestic agendas.

How will the new approach be received in Southeast Asia? Over the past four years, the US's standing in the region was undercut by indifference and ineptitude emanating from the highest levels. The next four years may be about climbing, rung by rung, out of the hole we have dug for ourselves.

Currently, there is much energy being spent and ink being spilled on this side of the Pacific wondering how best to regain an American claim to world leadership or whether it is even still possible.[35] I'd say that's the wrong question. Instead of fretting about leadership, the focus for the time being should be on contributing and partnering. This affords the opportunity to stand shoulder to shoulder with nations around the world to address shared problems. Our contributions will be greater in many cases, simply because our resources and capacity are more expansive, that's a given. But if we aspire to the privilege of being known as first among equals, it might be time to double down on the equals part for a while.

I started writing the essays in this book to try to make sense of chaotic times. As I explored policy connections with Southeast Asia, I found inspiration in the examples of so many people working tirelessly and fighting bravely for democratic reform there. There is work to be done in the US as well. Democracy is never a final destination. It is always a work in progress, and complacency is its enemy. Instances of harmony will provide a vision of what is possible, but we must be prepared to sit with the dissonance.

Subject Index

Acknowledgments

There have been many, many individuals in various countries who have shared their thoughts on politics and culture with me in innumerable encounters over the years. All of them have helped me gain a better understanding of Southeast Asia and I am grateful. I am equally indebted to the daily immersion in politics and policy afforded by my work and life in Washington, DC, and to the colleagues who help me remember that this work matters to people's lives.

Even a small book like this one requires many steps to come to fruition. Thanks to Bruce and Justine for putting the pages between two covers and sending it out to the wider world. Thanks also to Alexandre and Javier for providing visual images.

Most particular thanks go to Nick, James, Minh and Martyn for first publishing some of these essays in Australia and for helping me understand that I might have something to say about these strange times that would resonate with others.

END NOTES

3. Doctor, My Eyes

1.Tanenhaus, Sam, and Jim Rutenberg. "Rand Paul's Mixed Inheritance." New York Times, January 25, 2014. https://www.nytimes.com/2014/01/26/us/politics/rand-pauls-mixed-inheritance.html.

2. Bump, Philip. "Rand Paul Will Literally Stand in the Way of Syria Attacks (Update: Maybe)." The Atlantic, September 4, 2013. https://www.theatlantic.com/politics/archive/2013/09/rand-paul-will-literally-stand-way-syria-attacks/311453/.

3. GovTrak. "Sen. Rand Paul." Accessed January 12, 2017. https://www.govtrack.us/congress/members/rand_paul/412492.

4. Walsh, Dierdre, and MJ Lee. "Trump wants Obamacare repeal 'quickly,' but Republicans aren't ready." CNN, January 10, 2017. https://edition.cnn.com/2017/01/10/politics/paul-ryan-obamacare-repeal-and-replace/index.html.

5. Haberman, Maggie, and Robert Pear. "Trump Tells Congress to Repeal and Replace Health Care Law 'Very Quickly'." New York Times, January 10, 2017. https://www.nytimes.com/2017/01/10/us/repeal-affordable-care-act-donald-trump.html.

6. Coronini-Cronberg, Sophie, and Wongsa Laohasiriwong, and Christian A. Gericke. "Health care utilisation under the 30-Baht Scheme among the urban poor in Mitrapap slum, Khon Kaen, Thailand: a cross-sectional study." International Journal for Equity in Health 6, no. 11 (2007): https://doi.org/10.1186/1475-9276-6-11.

7. Everett, Burgess. "Paul, Trump upend GOP's Obamacare repeal plans." Politico, January 9, 2017. https://www.politico.com/story/2017/01/obamacare-repeal-trump-rand-paul-233351.

4. A Good Day's Work

1. Alexander, S., Véronique Salze-Lozac'h, and Arpaporn Winijkulchai. "Thailand Adopts Nationwide Minimum Wage Policy Amid Controversy." Asia Foundation, January 30, 2013. https://asiafoundation.org/2013/01/30/thailand-adopts-nationwide-minimum-wage-policy-amid-controversy/.

2. United States Department of Labor. "Minimum Wage Laws in the States." Accessed January 30, 2013. https://www.dol.gov/whd/minwage/america.htm.

3.Scheiber, Noam. "Trump's Labor Pick, Andrew Puzder, Is Critic of Minimum Wage Increases." New York Times, December 8, 2016. https://www.nytimes.com/2016/12/08/us/politics/andrew-puzder-labor-secretary-trump.html.

4. Faulders, Katherine, and Lissette Rodriguez. "Trump's Labor Secretary Pick Andrew Puzder Admits to Employing Undocumented Worker." ABC News, February 7, 2017. http://abcnews.go.com/Politics/trumps-labor-secretary-pick-andrew-puzder-admits-employing/story?id=45314474.

5. Puzzanghera, Jim. "Top Senate Democrat calls on Trump to withdraw Labor nominee Puzder." Los Angeles Times, February 9, 2017. http://www.latimes.com/politics/washington/la-na-essential-washington-updates-schumer-calls-on-trump-to-withdraw-1486663210-htmlstory.html.

6. Anna Lappé. "100+ Food and AG Groups Stand with Labor and Tell Senators to Vote No on Andy Puzder Nomination." Last modified January 30, 2017. https://annalappe.com/2017/01/100-food-ag-groups-stand-labor-tell-senators-vote-no-andy-puzder-nomination/.

7. "3 years on from Rana Plaza, the Bangladesh Accord is saving lives." IndustriALL Global Union, April 21, 2016. http://www.industriall-union.org/3-years-on-from-rana-plaza-the-bangladesh-accord-is-saving-lives.

5. Lock Them All Up

1. Martínez Cantera, Ángel L. "Inside the Philippine prison without walls." Southeast Asia Globe, January 10, 2017. http://www.sea-globe.com/Philippine-prison-without-walls.

2. Katz, Andrew. "This Photograph Makes Life Inside a Philippines Jail Look Like Dante's 'Inferno'." Time, August 3, 2016. http://www.time.com/4438112/philippines-overcrowded-prison-manila-rodrigo-duterte/.

3. Rauhala, Emily. "Philippines' Duterte backs bill lowering age of criminal responsibility to 9 years old." The Star (Toronto), February 26, 2017. https://www.thestar.com/news/world/2017/02/26/philippines-duterte-backs-bill-lowering-age-of-criminal-responsibility-to-9-years-old.html.

4. UNICEF. "UNICEF statement on calls to lower the age of criminal responsibility." Accessed March 16, 2017. https://www.unicef.org/philippines/media_25645.htm#.WMHlh2-GOUk.

5. The Royal Society. "Brain waves." Accessed March 16, 2017. https://royalsociety.org/topics-policy/projects/brain-waves/.

6. House of Representatives, Republic of the Philippines. "House Bill No. 002." Accessed March 16, 2017. http://www.congress.gov.ph/legisdocs/basic_17/HB00002.pdf.

7. Laird, Lorelei. "States raising age for adult prosecution back to 18." ABA Journal, February 1, 2017. http://www.abajournal.com/magazine/article/adult_prosecution_juvenile_justice.

8. The White House. "Fact Sheet: Enhancing the Fairness and Effectiveness of the Criminal Justice System." Last modified July 14, 2015. https://obamawhitehouse.archives.gov/the-press-office/2015/07/14/fact-sheet-enhancing-fairness-and-effectiveness-criminal-justice-system.

9. Carissimo, Justin. "Jeff Sessions reverses Obama order to phase out private prisons." Independent (UK), February 23, 2017. http://www.independent.co.uk/news/world/americas/jeff-sessions-signals-support-for-private-prisons-a7596661.html.

10. Beech, Eric. "U.S. reverses Obama-era move to phase out private prisons." Reuters, February 23, 2017. http://www.reuters.com/article/usa-prisons-idUSL1N1G82FP.

11. Takei, Carl. "Happy Birthday to the Corrections Corporation of America? Thirty Years of Banking on Bondage Leaves Little to Celebrate." American Civil Liberties Union, January 29, 2013. https://www.aclu.org/blog/happy-birthday-corrections-corporation-america-thirty-years-banking-bondage-leaves-little.

12. Children's Defense Fund. "Cradle to Prison Pipeline® Fact Sheet." Last modified October 1, 2009. http://www.childrensdefense.org/library/data/cradle-to-prison-pipeline-overview-fact-sheet-2009.pdf.

6. A Fashionable Entry to Policy?

1. Asia Islamic Fashion Week. http://www.asiaislamicfashionweek.com/.

2. Veridiano, Ruby. "At New York Fashion Week, 'Modest Fashion' Designer Makes Statement with Immigrant Models." NBC News, February 15, 2017. http://www.nbcnews.com/news/asian-america/new-york-fashion-week-modest-fashion-designer-makes-statement-immigrant-n720956.

3. Democratic Staff of the Joint Economic Committee, United States Congress. "The Economic Impact of the Fashion Industry." Last modified September 1, 2015. https://www.jec.senate.gov/public/_cache/files/2523ae10-9f05-4b8a-8954-631192dcd77f/jec-fashion-industry-report----sept-2015-update.pdf.

4. Kohen, Yael. "Will Ivanka Trump's Brand Be Even Bigger Without Ivanka? (It's Complicated)." Refinery29, March 7, 2017. http://www.refinery29.com/2017/03/142713/ivanka-trump-brand-reputation-sales-trump-inauguration.

5. Varinsky, Dana. "Ivanka Trump's foreign manufacturing practices could be her brand's next big headache." Business Insider, February 5, 2017. http://www.businessinsider.com/ivanka-trump-clothing-line-made-in-china-hong-kong-2017-2.

6. Levy, Gabrielle. "Al Gore: Ivanka Trump Concerned About Climate Change." U.S. News & World Report, December 6, 2016. https://www.usnews.com/news/politics/articles/2016-12-06/al-gore-ivanka-trump-concerned-about-climate-change.

7. Cotton Campaign. "Uzbekistan's Forced Labor problem." Accessed March 30, 2017. http://www.cottoncampaign.org/uzbekistans-forced-labor-problem.html.

7. The Taxman Cometh

1. Associated Press. "IRS is about to start using private debt collectors." Los Angeles Times, April 4, 2017. http://www.latimes.com/business/la-fi-irs-debt-collectors-20170404-story,amp.html.

2. . Pani, Priyanka. "GST: Amazon India worried about 'Tax Collection at Source' plan." Hindu Business Line, March 17, 2017. https://www.thehindubusinessline.com/info-tech/gst-amazon-india-worried-about-tax-collection-at-source-plan/article9589717.ece.

3. Sokheng, Vong, and Charles Rollet. "Assembly passes budget as CNRP boycotts vote." Phnom Penh Post, December 1, 2015. https://www.phnompenhpost.com/national/assembly-passes-budget-cnrp-boycotts-vote.

4. Maulia, Erwida, and Kiran Sharma. "How India and Indonesia are chasing tax revenue." Financial Times, December 25, 2016. https://www.ft.com/content/28141116-c841-11e6-8f29-9445cac8966f.

5. Franklin, Dallas. "Oklahoma Congressman: "You say you pay for me to do this? That's bullcrap, I pay for myself"." KFOR Oklahoma, April 12, 2017. http://kfor.com/2017/04/12/oklahoma-congressman-you-say-you-pay-for-me-to-do-this-thats-bullcrap-i-pay-for-myself-to-do-this/.

6. Paletta, Damian. "Trump budget expected to seek historic contraction of federal workforce." Washington Post, March 12, 2017. https://www.washingtonpost.com/business/economy/through-his-budget-a-bottom-line-look-at-trumps-new-washington/2017/03/12/29739206-05be-11e7-b9fa-ed727b644a0b_story.html?utm_term=.cd713bbf2ebb.

8. America First in the Final Frontier

1. Frank, Adam. "Science And Facts, Alternative Or Otherwise." NPR, January 24, 2017. https://www.npr.org/sections/13.7/2017/01/24/511348618/science-and-facts-alternative-or-otherwise.

2. Kahn, Brian, and Bobby Magill. "A Trump Budget Could Decimate Climate Funding." Climate Central. June 3, 2017. http://www.climatecentral.org/news/trump-budget-climate-funding-20907/.

3. Davis, Jason. "Trump's first budget proposal is out. Here's how NASA fared." The Planetary Society, March 16, 2017. http://www.planetary.org/blogs/jason-davis/2017/20170306-trumps-first-nasa-budget.html.

4. Smith, Marcia. "Trump: 'I Will Free NASA' from Being Just a LEO Space Logistics Agency." Space Policy Online, October 25, 2016. https://spacepolicyonline.com/news/trump-i-will-free-nasa-from-being-just-a-leo-space-logistics-agency/.

5. McFarland, Matt. "SpaceX to fly two space tourists around the moon in 2018." CNN Tech, February 27, 2017. http://money.cnn.com/2017/02/27/technology/spacex-moon-tourism/.

6. O'Brien, Miles. "California millionaire to go on $20 million ride to space station." CNN, January 26, 2001. http://edition.cnn.com/2001/TECH/space/01/26/tito.mir/index.html.

7. Gallucci, Nicole. "Donald Trump just got trolled from the 'first protest in space'." Mashable, April 13, 2017. http://mashable.com/2017/04/13/trump-trolled-tweet-stratosphere/#dTiNxM26sPq8.

8. University of Pennsylvania. "Psychologists study intense awe astronauts feel viewing Earth from space." ScienceDaily, April 19, 2016. www.sciencedaily.com/releases/2016/04/160419120055.htm.

9. Space Exploration Asia. "Space Exploration Asia." Accessed April 20, 2017. https://www.spaceexploration.asia/.

9. Busting the Model Minority Myth

1. Library of Congress and the National Archives and Records Administration, National Endowment for the Humanities, National Gallery of Art, National Park Service, Smithsonian Institution, and United States Holocaust Memorial Museum. "Asian/Pacific American Heritage Month." Accessed May 29, 2017. http://asianpacificheritage.gov/.

2. "CAPAC Members Mark 135th Anniversary of the Chinese Exclusion Act." Congressional Asian Pacific American Caucus, May 5, 2017. https://capac-chu. house.gov/press-release/capac-members-mark-135th-anniversary-chinese-exclusion-act.

3. Chow, Kat. "'Model Minority' Myth Again Used As A Racial Wedge Between Asians And Blacks." NPR, April 19, 2017. http://www.npr.org/sections/codeswitch/2017/04/19/524571669/model-minority-myth-again-used-as-a-racial-wedge-between-asians-and-blacks/.

4. Pew Research Center. "Asian Americans." Accessed May 29, 2017. http://www.pewsocialtrends.org/asianamericans-graphics/.

5. Chang, Sharon H. "The Growing Poverty Crisis That Everyone Is Ignoring." ThinkProgress, September 26, 2015. https://thinkprogress.org/the-growing-poverty-crisis-that-everyone-is-ignoring-f903e9200d32.

6. United States Census Bureau. "The Asian population: 2010." Last modified March 1, 2012. https://www.census.gov/prod/cen2010/briefs/c2010br-11.pdf.

7. Henderson, Wade. "Penny wise, pound foolish: 2020 Census needs funding now." The Hill, March 6, 2017. http://thehill.com/blogs/pundits-blog/the-administration/322503-penny-wise-pound-foolish-2020-census-needs-funding-now.

8. Maciag, Michael. "Without More Census Funding, Disadvantaged Communities Risk Being Overlooked Most." Governing, May 15, 2017. http://www.governing.com/topics/politics/gov-2020-census-funding-debate.html.

9. Jones, Robert P., Daniel Cox, and Rachel Lienesch. "Beyond Economics: Fears of Cultural Displacement Pushed the White Working Class to Trump." PRRI | The Atlantic, May 9, 2017. https://www.prri.org/research/white-working-class-attitudes-economy-trade-immigration-election-donald-trump/.

10. On Second Thought, You Can Keep Your Huddled Masses

1. Daley, Jason. "Haunting Twitter Account Shares the Fates of the Refugees of the St. Louis." Smithsonian, January 27, 2017. http://www.smithsonianmag.com/smart-news/haunting-twitter-account-shares-the-fates-of-the-refugees-of-st-louis-180961955.

2. American Immigration Council. "An Overview of U.S. Refugee Law and Policy." Accessed January 27, 2017. https://www.americanimmigrationcouncil.org/research/overview-us-refugee-law-and-policy.

3. Felter, Claire, and James McBride. "How Does the U.S. Refugee System Work?" Council on Foreign Relations, October 10, 2018. https://www.cfr.org/backgrounder/how-does-us-refugee-system-work.

4. Binckes, Jeremy. "Donald Trump may have undermined his administration's travel ban defense." Salon, June 5, 2017. http://www.salon.com/2017/06/05/donald-trump-may-have-undermined-his-administrations-travel-ban-defense.
5. United States Courts. "Judicial Vacancies." Accessed June 5, 2017. http://www.uscourts.gov/judges-judgeships/judicial-vacancies.

6. Daniel, Zoe, and Stephanie March. "US refugee deal: Architect of deal says arrangement loosely based on Australia 'doing more'." ABC News (Australia), March 21, 2017. http://www.abc.net.au/news/2017-03-22/us-refugee-deal-architect-says-based-on-australia-doing-more/8375250.

7. Disis, Jill, and Cristina Alesci. "The controversial visa program at the center of the Kushners' China pitch." CNN Money, May 11, 2017. http://money.cnn.com/2017/05/11/news/economy/china-kushner-eb5-program/index.html.

8. Townsend, Mark. "Far right raises £50,000 to target boats on refugee rescue missions in Med." The Guardian, June 3, 2017. https://www.theguardian.com/world/2017/jun/03/far-right-raises-50000-target-refugee-rescue-boats-med.

11. Blurring the Lines Between Church and State

1. Green, Emma. "The Supreme Court Strikes Down a Major Church-State Barrier." The Atlantic, June 26, 2017. https://www.theatlantic.com/politics/archive/2017/06/trinity-lutheran/531399.

2. Gilbert, Lisa. "Financial Services Appropriations Legislation Is a Right-Wing Wish List." Public Citizen, June 29, 2017. https://www.citizen.org/media/press-releases/financial-services-appropriations-legislation-right-wing-wish-list.

3. Moore, Mark. "Trump mocks Schwarzenegger, 'Apprentice' ratings at prayer breakfast." New York Post, February 2, 2017. https://nypost.com/2017/02/02/trump-mocks-schwarzenegger-apprentice-ratings-at-prayer-breakfast/.

4. Frazier, Kelly. "'No religion' tops religious affiliation poll in Australia." World Religion News, June 28, 2017. https://www.worldreligionnews.com/religion-news-/no-religion-tops-religious-affiliation-poll-australia.

5. Lipka, Michael. "5 facts about Catholicism in the Philippines." Pew Research Center, January 9, 2015. http://www.pewresearch.org/fact-tank/2015/01/09/5-facts-about-catholicism-in-the-philippines/.

6. Dialectic.sg. "Should the finances of religious organisations be more strictly regulated?" Singapore Policy Journal, October 26, 2015. https://singaporepolicyjournal.com/2015/10/26/should-the-finances-of-religious-organisations-be-more-strictly-regulated.

7. Ohlheiser, Abby. "Pastor Creflo Dollar might get his $65 million private jet after all." Washington Post, June 3, 2015. https://www.washingtonpost.com/news/acts-of-faith/wp/2015/06/03/pastor-creflo-dollar-might-get-his-65-million-private-jet-after-all/?utm_term=.602e19fac3ec.

8. Taylor, Jim. "The perplexing case of Wat Dhammakaya." New Mandala, March 16, 2017. http://www.newmandala.org/perplexing-case-wat-dhammakaya/.

9. Stetzer, Ed. "Southern Baptists, Racism, and the Alt-Right: It's Time to Make This Right, Plain, and Clear." Christianity Today, June 15, 2017. http://www.christianitytoday.com/edstetzer/2017/june/southern-baptists-racism-alt-right-five-things-you-need-to-.html.

10. Phillip, Abby, John Wagner, and Michael Birnbaum. "Western values increasingly endangered by terrorism and extremism, Trump warns Europe." Washington Post, July 6, 2017. https://www.washingtonpost.com/news/post-politics/wp/2017/07/06/in-poland-trump-reaffirms-commitment-to-nato-chides-russia/?utm_term=.2f831ed48866.

12. 'Shall We Dance' with Censorship or Free Expression?

1. Culwell-Block, Logan. "A History of Casting King and I — Cultural Evolution and Community Action." Playbill, April 26, 2015. http://www.playbill.com/article/a-history-of-casting-king-and-i-cultural-evolution-and-community-action-com-346584.

2. Buruma, Ian. "Thailand's Banned 'King'." New York Review of Books, May 19, 2015. http://www.nybooks.com/daily-2015/05/19/thailands-banned-king-and-i/?printpage=true.

3. Rattanasengchanh, Phimmasone M. "Thailands Second Triumvirate: Sarit Thanarat and the Military, King Bhumibol Adulyadej and the Monarchy and the United States. 1957-1963." Master's thesis, University of Washington, 2012. https://digital.lib.washington.edu/researchworks/bitstream/handle/1773/21997/Rattanasengchanh_washington_0250O_10615.pdf?sequence=1.

4. Free Republic. "His Majesty The King's Birthday Speech (Thailand)." Last modified December 5, 2005. http://www.freerepublic.com/focus/news/1534028/posts.

5. Phaicharoen, Nontarat. "Thai Court Sentences Man to 35-Year Prison Term for Insulting Monarchy." Benar News, June 9, 2017. http://www.benarnews.org/english/news/thai/thailand-monarchy-06092017163302.html.

6. "Thai lese majeste laws extended to viewing of insulting content." Straits Times, May 23, 2017. http://www.straitstimes.com/asia/se-asia/thai-lese-majeste-laws-extended-to-viewing-of-insulting-content.

7. Kludt, Tom. "Trump calls for changes to libel laws in attack on New York Times." CNN, March 30, 2017. http://money.cnn.com/2017/03/30/media/libel-laws-donald-trump-new-york-times/index.html.

8. Walden, Max. "Trump Instagram mistakes Singapore's Lee for Indonesia's Jokowi." Asian Correspondent, July 10, 2017. https://asiancorrespondent.com/2017/07/trump-instagram-mistakes-singapores-lee-indonesias-jokowi/#RSujZvRWMj93Z7Ca.97.

9. Turner Garrison, Laura. "The Moustache Brothers and the Risky Act of Doing Comedy in Burma." Vulture. April 13, 2011. https://www.vulture.com/2011/04/the-moustache-brothers-and-the-risky-act-of-doing-comedy-in-burma.html.

13. Exporting Addiction

1. Moodley, Kiran. "Welcome to the Golden Triangle, the centre of the world's drug trafficking." Independent (UK), March 11, 2015. http://www.independent.co.uk/news/world/asia/welcome-to-the-golden-triangle-the-centre-of-the-worlds-drug-trafficking-10100420.html.

2. Katz, Josh. "Drug Deaths in America Are Rising Faster Than Ever." New York Times, June 5, 2017. http://www.nytimes.com/interactive/2017/06/05/upshot/opioid-epidemic-drug-overdose-deaths-are-rising-faster-than-ever.html?mcub2=1.

3. Kamarulzaman, Adeeba, and John L. McBrayer. "Compulsory drug detention centers in East and Southeast Asia." The International Journal on Drug Policy 26, no. 1 Suppl (Feb 2015): S33-37, https://doi.org/10.1016/j.drugpo.2014.11.011

4. "Commission on Combating Drug Addiction and the Opioid Crisis Interim Report." Letter to President of the United States Donald Trump. 2017. In The White House. https://www.whitehouse.gov/sites/whitehouse.gov/files/ondcp/commission-interim-report.pdf.

5. "Duterte forms task force to create, support drug rehab centers." Philippine Star, October 16, 2016. http://www.philstar.com/headlines/2016/10/16/1634069/duterte-forms-task-force-create-support-drug-rehab-centers.

6. Weiss, Brennan. "How to rehabilitate addicts in the Philippines' vicious drug war?" Public Radio International, April 11, 2017. https://www.pri.org/stories/2017-04-11/how-rehabilitate-addicts-philippines-vicious-drug-war.

7. The White House. "Remarks by President Trump Before a Briefing on the Opioid Crisis." Last modified August 8, 2017. https://www.whitehouse.gov/the-press-office/2017/08/08/remarks-president-trump-briefing-opioid-crisis.

8. Ryan, Harriet, Lisa Girion, and Scott Glover. "OxyContin goes global — "We're only just getting started"." Los Angeles Times, December 18, 2016. http://www.latimes.com/projects/la-me-oxycontin-part3/.

9. "Re: Mundipharma International." Letter to Dr. Margaret Chan, Director-General, World Health Organization. May 3, 2017. In U.S. Congresswoman Katherine Clark. http://www.katherineclark.house.gov/_cache/files/a577bd3c-29ec-4bb9-bdba-1ca71c784113/mundipharma-letter-signatures.pdf.

14. The Art of Pushing Pills

1. Harris, Elizabeth A. "The Louvre Took Down the Sackler Name. Here's Why Other Museums Probably Won't." New York Times, July 18, 2019. https://www.nytimes.com/2019/07/18/arts/sackler-family-museums.html.

2. Gelineau, Kristin. "Opioid Crisis Goes Global as Deaths Surge in Australia." AP News, September 5, 2019. https://apnews.com/article/us-news-ap-top-news-opioids-international-news-health-cfc86f47e03843849a89ab3fce44c73c.

3. Lurie, Julia. "The Purdue Settlement is a Great Deal—for the Sacklers." Mother Jones, September 23, 2019. https://www.motherjones.com/politics/2019/09/the-purdue-settlement-is-a-great-deal-for-the-sacklers/.

4. Miller, Jake. "Dramatic Shifts in First Time Opioid Prescriptions Drop by 50 Percent" Harvard Gazette, March 13, 2019. https://news.harvard.edu/gazette/story/2019/03/dramatic-shifts-in-first-time-opioid-prescriptions-bring-hope-concern/.

5. Goodnough, Abby, Josh Katz, and Margot Sanger-Katz. "Drug Overdose Deaths Drop in U.S. for First Time Since 1990." New York Times, July 17, 2019. https://www.nytimes.com/interactive/2019/07/17/upshot/drug-overdose-deaths-fall.html.

6. Stobbe, Mike. "Decline in Opioid Deaths is Tied to Growing Use of Over-dose-reversing Drug, CDC Says." Los Angeles Times, August 6, 2019. https://www.latimes.com/science/story/2019-08-06/soaring-use-of-naloxone-tied-to-decline-in-opioid-deaths.

7. Freudenberger, Erica. "Not Just Narcan." Library Journal, May 7, 2019. https://www.libraryjournal.com/?detailStory=Not-Just-Narcan.

8. Varney, Sarah. "Beset by Lawsuits and Criticism in U.S., Opioid Makers Eye New Market in India." Kaiser Health News, August 28, 2019. https://khn.org/news/india-burgeoning-chronic-pain-market-us-drugmakers-stand-to-profit/.

9. Carvalho, Raquel. "Fentanyl Chemists are Getting Creative: Here's How China Plans to Stop the Flow of Deadly Drugs." South China Morning Post, December 4, 2018. https://www.scmp.com/week-asia/geopolitics/article/2176358/fentanyl-chemists-are-getting-creative-heres-how-china-plans.

10. Pardo, Bryce. "Some Asian Nations Reforming Drug Policies, China Un-likely to Curb Fentanyl Exports in Short Term." RAND Corporation, May 15, 2019. https://www.rand.org/news/press/2019/05/15.html.

11. "Philippines: President Duterte's Fierce Rival Becomes New Drug Czar." BBC, November 6, 2019. http://www.bbc.com/news/world-asia-50313866.

12. Blackman, Kate. "Opioid Policy Trends Continue in 2018 Legislative Sessions." National Conference of State Legislators, September 12, 2018. https://www.ncsl.org/blog/2018/09/12/opioid-policy-trends-continue-in-2018-legislative-sessions.aspx.

13. Sarlin, Eric. "A Promising Alternative to Opioid Pain Modifications." National Institute on Drug Abuse (NIDA) Notes, February 12, 2019. https://www.drugabuse.gov/news-events/nida-notes/2019/02/promising-alternative-to-opioid-pain-medications.

15. Where There's Smoke, There's Coal

1. Mufson, Steven, and Chris Mooney. "Rick Perry just proposed sweeping new steps to help struggling coal and nuclear plants." Washington Post, September 29, 2017. https://www.washingtonpost.com/news/energy-environment/wp/2017/09/29/rick-perry-proposes-sweeping-new-moves-to-support-coal-and-nuclear-plants/?utm_term=.f42caeeb6.

2. Farmer, Miles. "DOE Proposes Outrageous, Massive Coal and Nuclear Bailout." Natural Resources Defense Council, September 29, 2017. https://www.nrdc.org/experts/miles-farmer/doe-proposes-outrageous-massive-coal-and-nuclear-bailout.

3. Possner, Anna, and Ken Caldeira. "Geophysical potential for wind energy over the open oceans." National Academy of Sciences 114, no. 43 (October 9, 2017): 11338-11343, https://doi.org/10.1073/pnas.1705710114.

4. United States Department of Energy. "Staff Report to the Secretary on Electricity Markets and Reliability." Last modified August 1, 2017. https://energy.gov/sites/prod/files/2017/08/f36/Staff Report on Electricity Markets and Reliability_0.pdf.

5. Friedman, Lisa, and Brad Plumer. "E.P.A. Announces Repeal of Major Obama-Era Carbon Emissions Rule." New York Times, October 9, 2017. https://www.nytimes.com/2017/10/09/climate/clean-power-plan.html.

6. Nguyen, Mai. "Formosa unit offers $500 million for causing toxic disaster in Vietnam." Reuters (UK), June 30, 2016. http://uk.reuters.com/article/us-vietnam-environment/formosa-unit-offers-500-million-for-causing-toxic-disaster-in-vietnam-idUKKCN0ZG1F5.

7. Clark, Helen. "Why Is Climate-Conscious Vietnam Choosing Coal Over Nuclear?" South China Morning Post, December 12, 2016. http://www.scmp.com/week-asia/business/article/2053399/why-climate-conscious-vietnam-choosing-coal-over-nuclear.

8. Nguyen, Viet Phuong. "With Growth of Coal Power Plants, Vietnam's Future Is Grim." The Diplomat, January 25, 2017. https://thediplomat.com/2017/01/with-growth-of-coal-power-plants-vietnams-future-is-grim/.

9. Koplitz, Shannon N., Daniel J. Jacob, Melissa P. Sulprizio, Lauri Myllyvirta, and Colleen Reid. "Burden of Disease from Rising Coal-Fired Power Plant Emissions in Southeast Asia." Environmental Science & Technology 51, no. 3 (2017): 1467-1476. https://doi.org/10.1021/acs.est.6b03731.

10. International Energy Agency. "World Energy Outlook Special Report on Southeast Asia 2015." Accessed October 13, 2017. https://www.iea.org/publications/freepublications/publication/world-energy-outlook-special-report-on-southeast-asia-2015.html.

17. The World as a Hostile Workplace

1. Farrow, Ronan. "From Aggressive Overtures to Sexual Assault: Harvey Weinstein's Accusers Tell Their Stories." New Yorker, October 23, 2017. https://www.newyorker.com/news/news-desk/from-aggressive-overtures-to-sexual-assault-harvey-weinsteins-accusers-tell-their-stories.

2. Dann, Carrie. "NBC/WSJ Poll: Nearly Half of Working Women Say They Have Experienced Harassment." NBC News, October 30, 2017. https://www.nbcnews.com/politics/first-read/nbc-wsj-poll-nearly-half-working-women-say-they-ve-n815376.

3. Global Labor Justice Report. "Gender Based Violence in the Walmart Garment Supply Chain." Last modified March 23, 2018. https://asia.floorwage.org/wp-content/uploads/2019/10/GBV-walmart.pdf.

4. WORLD Policy Analysis Center - UCLA Fielding School of Public Health. "Preventing Gender-Based Workplace Discrimination and Sexual Harassment: New Data on 193 Countries." Accessed June 4, 2018. https://www.worldpolicycenter.org/sites/default/files/WORLD Discrimination at Work Report.pdf.

5. 107th Session of the International Labor Conference, Resolution, Standard Setting Committee: Violence and Harassment in the World of Work, July 6, 2018

18. Diversity or Discrimination May Be in the Eye of the Beholder

1. Gluckman, Nell. "Harvard's Race-Conscious Admissions Policy Goes on Trial on Monday. Here's What to Expect." Chronicle of Higher Education, October 12, 2018. https://www.chronicle.com/article/harvards-race-conscious-admissions-policy-goes-on-trial-on-monday-heres-what-to-expect/.

2. Asian Americans Advancing Justice. "Asian Americans Advancing Justice Files Brief in Support of Race-Conscious Admissions at Harvard." Last modified July 30, 2018. https://advancingjustice-aajc.org/press-release/asian-americans-advancing-justice-files-brief-support-race-conscious-admissions.

3. Lockhart, P.R. "The Lawsuit Against Harvard that Could Change Affirmative Action in College Admissions, Explained." Vox, October 18, 2018. https://www.vox.com/2018/10/18/17984108/harvard-asian-americans-affirmative-action-racial-discrimination.

4. Benner, Katie. "Justice Dept. Backs Suit Accusing Harvard of Discriminating Against Asian American Students." New York Times, August 30, 2018. https://www.nytimes.com/2018/08/30/us/politics/asian-students-affirmative-action-harvard.html.

5. Chin, James. "How Dr. M Can Tackle Malaysia's Bumiputera Policy." Free Malaysia Today, May 14, 2018. https://www.freemalaysiatoday.com/category/opinion/2018/05/14/how-dr-m-can-tackle-malaysias-bumiputera-policy/?__cf_chl_jschl_tk__=pmd_OTcHLeXAAbHkbM2hX4BGundRVNfqd3EQRdT4fYPQrSE-1630539446-0-gqNtZGzNAnujcnBszQil.

6. Tan, C.K. "Mahathir Advisers Propose Review of Malay Privileges to Spur Economy." Nikkei Asia, August 20, 2018. https://asia.nikkei.com/Politics/Malaysia-in-transition/Mahathir-advisers-propose-review-of-Malay-privileges-to-spur-economy.

19. Strangers in a Strange Land

1. Yong, Charissa. "US Hardens Stance on Immigration, Ramps Up Efforts to Deport Vietnam War Refugees." Straits Times, December 19, 2018. https://www.straitstimes.com/world/united-states/us-hardens-stance-on-immigration-ramps-up-efforts-to-deport-vietnam-war-refugees.

2. Gross, Daniel. "A Cambodian Refugee with a Decades Old Conviction and a Pregnant Wife Fights Deportation." New Yorker, December 17, 2018. https://www.newyorker.com/news/as-told-to/cambodian-refugee-with-a-decades-old-conviction-and-a-pregnant-wife-fights-deportation.

3. Elias, Paul. "California High Court Blocks Pardon of Cambodian Refugee Who Killed at 14." Mercury News, December 17, 2018. https://www.mercurynews.com/2018/12/17/california-high-court-blocks-pardon-of-man-who-killed-at-14/.

4. Lee, Elizabeth. "Cambodian-Americans Flex a Long-Silent Voice in US Midterm Elections." VOA, November 2, 2018. https://www.voanews.com/usa/us-politics/cambobian-americans-flex-long-silent-voice-us-midterm-elections.

20. If Hong Kong Can Have Democracy, Then Why Not the US?

1. Hong Kong Human Rights and Democracy Act of 2019, H.R. 3289, 116th Cong. (2019).

2. Carney, Jordain. "McConnell urges Trump to voice support for Hong Kong protesters." The Hill, November 18, 2019. https://thehill.com/blogs/floor-action/senate/471019-mcconnell-urges-trump-to-voice-support-for-hong-kong-protesters.

3. DC Statehood. "Home." Accessed December 19, 2019. https://statehood.dc.gov/.

4. Harris, Wiltshire & Grannis LLP. "HWG Argues D.C. Voting Rights Case Before Special Three-Judge Panel in U.S. District Court." Last modified November 26, 2019. https://www.hwglaw.com/hwg-argues-d-c-voting-rights-case-before-special-three-judge-panel-in-u-s-district-court/.

5. Greenblatt, Alan. "The US almost tore itself apart to get to 50 states. Can DC make it 51?" Vox, June 5, 2020. https://www.vox.com/the-highlight/2019/9/18/20863026/dc-statehood-george-floyd-puerto-rico-statehood.

6. Urbina, Ian. "Senators Tie Gun Issue to Capital-Vote Bill." New York Times, February 27, 2009. https://www.nytimes.com/2009/02/27/us/politics/27district.html.

7. Martin, Nick. "The Argument Against D.C. Statehood Is Rooted in Racism." New Republic, September 20, 2019. https://newrepublic.com/article/155132/racist-roots-dc-statehood.

8. Marquette, Chris. "New hearing on D.C. statehood, same old partisan lines." Roll Call, September 19, 2019. https://www.rollcall.com/2019/09/19/new-hearing-on-d-c-statehood-same-old-partisan-lines/

21. Strongman Politics in a Crisis

1. Wells, Spencer. "Singapore is the Model for How to Handle the Coronavirus." MIT Technology Review, March 12, 2020. https://www.technologyreview.com/2020/03/12/905346/singapore-is-the-model-for-how-to-handle-the-coronavirus/.

2. Carlson, Margaret. "Trump is Raving, Fauci is Losing and the Virus is Winning." Daily Beast, March 25, 2020. https://www.thedailybeast.com/trump-is-raving-fauci-is-losing-and-the-virus-is-winning.

3. Aspinwall, Nick. "Coronavirus Lockdown Launches Manila Into Pandemonium", Foreign Policy, March 14, 2020. https://foreignpolicy.com/2020/03/14/duterte-quarantine-philippines-coronavirus-lockdown-launches-manila-into-pandemonium/.

4. McCarthy, Julie. "Concerns in Philippines After Duterte Given Emergency Powers to Fight COVID-19 Spread", NPR, March 24, 2020. https://www.npr.org/sections/coronavirus-live-updates/2020/03/24/820906636/concerns-in-philippines-after-duterte-given-emergency-powers-to-fight-covid-19-s.

5. Human Rights Watch. "Thailand: COVID-19 Clampdown on Free Speech." Last modified March 25, 2020. https://www.hrw.org/news/2020/03/25/thailand-covid-19-clampdown-free-speech.

6. Stillman, Jessica. "Got a Hard Decision to Make? Borrow Obama's Simple 3-Part Strategy for the Toughest Calls." Inc. Magazine, March 8, 2019. https://www.inc.com/jessica-stillman/president-obama-just-shared-his-simple-3-part-framework-for-making-even-toughest-decisions.html.

7. Dreid, Nadia. "Immigrants Cut Out of Senate's COVID-19 Stimulus Package." Law 360, March 26, 2020. https://www.law360.com/tax-authority/articles/1257333/immigrants-cut-out-of-senate-s-covid-19-stimulus-package.

8. "Indonesian Migrants in Malaysia 'Going Hungry' During Movement Control Order." New Straits Times, March 28, 2020. https://www.nst.com.my/news/nation/2020/03/579214/indonesian-migrants-malaysia-going-hungry-during-mco.

22. 'Stay Safe' Is an Empty Platitude in a World Riddled by Inequality

1. "Curfew Imposed in 40 Cities Including Washington, DC as Protests Spread Across the US." WIO News, June 1, 2020. https://www.wionews.com/world/curfew-imposed-in-40-cities-including-washington-dc-as-protests-spread-across-us-302235.

2. Sprunt, Barbara. "The History Behind 'When the Looting Starts, the Shooting Starts'." NPR, May 29, 2020. https://www.npr.org/2020/05/29/864818368/the-history-behind-when-the-looting-starts-the-shooting-starts.

3. "'Shoot Them Dead' – Philippine Leader Says Won't Tolerate Lockdown Violators." Reuters, April 1, 2020. https://www.reuters.com/article/us-health-coronavirus-philippines-dutert/shoot-them-dead-philippine-leader-says-wont-tolerate-lockdown-violators-idUSKBN21K0AY.

4. Raymond, Adam K. "Trump Calls Governors 'Weak,' Tells Them to 'Dominate' Protesters." New York Magazine, June 1, 2020. https://nymag.com/intelligencer/2020/06/trump-tells-weak-governors-to-dominate-protesters.html.

5. "Officials Blame Differing Groups of 'Outsiders' for Violence Across U.S." CBS Minnesota, May 30, 2020. https://minnesota.cbslocal.com/2020/05/30/officials-blame-differing-groups-of-outsiders-for-violence-across-u-s/.

6. Gupta, Sujata. "Why African-Americans May Be Especially Vulnerable to COVID-19", Science News, April 10, 2020. https://www.sciencenews.org/article/coronavirus-why-african-americans-vulnerable-covid-19-health-race.

7. Melley, Brian, and John Seewer. "US Cities Fear Protest May Fuel Coronavirus Outbreaks." Associated Press, May 30, 2020. https://apnews.com/article/united-nations-health-minnesota-ap-top-news-virus-outbreak-ae27c6f51e97f4eaddb528b3f5027848.

8. Ramzy, Austin. "Hong Kong Bans Tiananmen Vigil for 1st Time, in New Challenge to Protests." New York Times, June 1, 2020. https://www.nytimes.com/2020/06/01/world/asia/Hong-kong-Tiananmen-vigil-banned.html.

9. "US and Allies Condemn China Over Hong Kong National Security Law." Al Jazeera, May 29, 2020. https://www.aljazeera.com/news/2020/5/29/us-and-allies-condemn-china-over-hong-kong-national-security-law.

10. Bismonte, Camille. "The Disproportionate Effect of COVID-19 on Migrant Workers in ASEAN." The Diplomat, May 22, 2020. https://thediplomat.com/2020/05/the-disproportionate-effect-of-covid-19-on-migrant-workers-in-asean/.

23. Children's Crusades

1. Haig, Christian Stirling, Katherine Schmidt, and Samuel Brannen. "The Age of Mass Protests: Understanding an Escalating Global Trend." CSIS Report, March 2, 2020. https://www.csis.org/analysis/age-mass-protests-understanding-escalating-global-trend.

2. Library of Congress. "Youth in the Civil Rights Movement." Accessed September 2, 2021. www.loc.gov/collections/civil-rights-history-project/articles-and-essays/youth-in-the-civil-rights-movement.

3. "Thailand Protests: Humor and Creativity Amid Repression." DW, November 25, 2020. www.dw.com/en/thailand-protests-humor-and-creativity-amid-repression/g-55721064.

4. "Protesters spatter blood on Thai PM's home." CNN, March 17, 2010. www.cnn.com/2010/WORLD/asiapcf/03/17/thailand.protests/index.html.

5. Ratcliffe, Rebecca. "Pro-democracy movement draws thousands in Bangkok." The Guardian, August 16, 2020. https://www.theguardian.com/world/2020/aug/16/thousands-call-for-reforms-to-monarchy-in-bangkok-protests.

6. Interview with Kunthida Rungruengkiat, April 2021

7. "March for Our Lives: Huge Gun Control Rallies Sweep US." BBC, March 24, 2018. http://www.bbc.com/news/world-us-canada-43526413.

8. STOP School Violence Act of 2018, H.R. 4909, 115th Cong. (2018).

9. Clarkson, Brett. "The 'online smear machine' that called Parkland students 'crisis actors' is Politifact's Lie of the Year." South Florida Sun Sentinel, December 11, 2018. www.sun-sentinel.com/local/broward/parkland/florida-school-shooting/fl-ne-politifact-biggest-lie-parkland-20181211-story.html.

10. "Army Chief Lashes Out at 'Nation Haters' 2 Days After Protest." Khaosod English, August 5, 2020. www.khaosodenglish.com/politics/2020/08/05/army-chief-lashes-out-at-nation-haters-2-days-after-protest.

11. Interview with Nuttaa Mahattana in March, 2021

12. Mahattana, Nuttaa. "The letter to my son: the injustice faced by an older brother, 'Pai'." Prachatai, February 2, 2017. https://prachatai.com/english/node/6894.

13. "Thailand's king seeks to bring back absolute monarchy." The Economist, October 14, 2020. www.economist.com/briefing/2020/10/14/thailands-king-seeks-to-bring-back-absolute-monarchy.

14. "Thai PM 'concerned' after student protest new demands on monarchy." Reuters, August 11, 2020. https://www.reuters.com/article/thailand-protests-idINKCN2570LW.

15. Center for Homeland Defense & Security. "K-12 School Shooting Database." Accessed September 3, 2021. https://www.chds.us/ssdb/.

16. State Firearm Laws. "State Firearm Laws Database." Accessed September 3, 2021. https://www.statefirearmlaws.org/state-state-firearm-law-data.

17. Hess, Abigail Johnson. "The 2020 Election Shows Gen Z's Voting Power for Years to Come." CNBC, November 18, 2020. http://www.cnbc.com/2020/11/18/the-2020-election-shows-gen-zs-voting-power-for-years-to-come.html.

24. Beyond Representation: Southeast Asian American Political Participation

1. Fuller, Thomas. "He came from Thailand to care for family. Then came brutal attack." New York Times, February 27, 2021. https://www.nytimes.com/2021/02/27/us/asian-american-hate-crimes.html.

2. Wang, Amy B. "Record Asian American turnout helped Biden win Georgia. Can it help flip the Senate?" Washington Post, November 28, 2020. https://www.washingtonpost.com/politics/asian-americans-georgia-senate/2020/11/28/28521068-2ad2-11eb-9b14-ad872157ebc9_story.html.

3. Interview with Madalene Xuan-Trang Mielke, February 2021

4. Asian and Pacific Islander American Vote. "2020 Asian American Voter Survey." Accessed September 3, 2021. https://www.apiavote.org/research/2020-asian-american-voter-survey.

5. Djou, Charles. "Why I'm Leaving the Republican Party." Honolulu Civil Beat, March 19, 2018. https://www.civilbeat.org/2018/03/charles-djou-why-im-leaving-the-gop/.

6. Interview with Darith Ung, April 2021

7. Kiley, Paula. "How the Cambodian-Americans dominated the Long Beach doughnut scene." Daily Forty-Niner, April 7, 2019. https://daily49er.com/artslife/2019/04/07/special-issue-how-cambodian-americans-dominated-the-long-beach-doughnut-scene/.

8. Interview with Sandy Dang, April 2021

9. Lao, Molly. "The case for requiring disaggregation of Asian American and Pacific Islander data." California Law Review, March 2021. https://www.californialawreview.org/the-case-for-requiring-disaggregation-of-asian-american-and-pacific-islander-data/.

10. Kochhar, Rakesh, and Anthony Cilluffo. "Income inequality in the US is rising most rapidly among Asians." Pew Research Center, July 12, 2018. https://www.pewresearch.org/social-trends/2018/07/12/income-inequality-in-the-u-s-is-rising-most-rapidly-among-asians/.

11. Wang, Hansi Lo. "'Racist bill'? Chinese immigrants protest effort to collect more Asian-American data." NPR, August 5, 2017. https://www.npr.org/2017/08/05/541844705/protests-against-the-push-to-disaggragate-asian-american-data.

12. Interview with Chinada Phaengdra Potter, April 2021

13. Yam, Kimmy. "Officer who stood by as George Floyd died highlights complex Asian American, black relations." NBC News, June 1, 2020. https://www.nbcnews.com/news/asian-america/officer-who-stood-george-floyd-died-asian-american-we-need-n1221311.

14. Moon, Kat. "Raya and the Last Dragon introduces Disney's first Southeast Asian princess. Advocates say Hollywood representation shouldn't stop there." TIME, March 5, 2021. https://time.com/5944583/raya-and-the-last-dragon-southeast-asia/ - :~:text=t Stop There-,Raya and the Last Dragon Introduces Disney's First Southeast Asian,Representation Shouldn't Stop There&text=The arrival of Raya,Asian.

15. Interview with Julie Diep, March 2021

16. Duckworth, Tammy. Every Day is a Gift: A Memoir. New York: Twelve/ Hachette Book Group, 2021.

17. Raju, Manu, and Clare Foran. "Two Asian American Senators back off of threat to oppose Biden nominees after White House agrees to add senior AAPI advisor." CNN, March 24, 2021. https://www.cnn.com/2021/03/23/politics/duckworth-hirono-aapi-nominees/index.html.

18. The White House. "Fact Sheet: President Biden announces additional actions to respond to anti-Asian violence, xenophobia and bias." Last modified March 30, 2021. https://www.whitehouse.gov/briefing-room/statements-releases/2021/03/30/fact-sheet-president-biden-announces-additional-actions-to-respond-to-anti-asian-violence-xenophobia-and-bias/.

25. What Lies Ahead

1. Lyons, Kate, Matthew Weaver, and Benjamin Haas. "Singapore Summit: what we learned from the Trump-Kim meeting." The Guardian, June 12, 2018. https://www.theguardian.com/world/2018/jun/12/singapore-meeting-what-we-know-so-far.

2. "Trump's top five withdrawals from international agreements." TRT World, June 29, 2018. www.trtworld.com/Americas/trump-s-top-five-withdrawals-from-international-agreements-18543.

3. Branswell, Helen. "Trump Administration submits formal notice of withdrawal from WHO." STAT, July 7, 2020. https://www.statnews.com/2020/07/07/trump-administration-submits-formal-notice-of-withdrawal-from-who/.

4. Tenpas, Kathryn Dunn. "Why is Trump's staff turnover higher than the 5 most recent presidents?" Brookings Institute, January 19, 2018. https://www.brookings.edu/research/why-is-trumps-staff-turnover-higher-than-the-5-most-recent-presidents/.

5. Cook, Malcolm. "Biden versus Trump in Southeast Asia: where the rubber meets the road." Asialink, May 11, 2021. www.asialink.unimelb.edu.au/insights/biden-versus-trump-in-southeast-asia-where-the-rubber-meets-the-road.

6. Strangio, Sebastian. "Amid Chinese Push, US Official to Visit Three Southeast Asian Nations." The Diplomat, May 25, 2021. https://thediplomat.com/2021/05/amid-chinese-push-us-official-to-visit-three-southeast-asian-nations/.

7. US Department of State. "Deputy Secretary of State Wendy Sherman's Visit to Cambodia." Last modified June 1, 2021. www.state.gov/deputy-secretary-of-state-wendy-shermans-visit-to-cambodia/.

8. Johnson, Kay, and Panarat Thepgumpanat. "Analysis: Myanmar's neighbor Thailand unlikely to toughen stance on coup." Reuters, April 2, 2021. https://www.reuters.com/article/us-myanmar-politics-thailand-analysis/analysis-myanmars-neighbour-thailand-unlikely-to-toughen-stance-on-coup-idUSKBN2BP0LN.

9. Septiari, Dian. "US lays on the charm, highlights Indo-Pacific values during Indonesian visit." The Jakarta Post, June 1, 2021. http://www.thejakartapost.com/news/2021/06/01/us-lays-on-the-charm-highlights-indo-pacific-values-during-ri-leg-of-sea-tour.html.

10. ASEAN Studies Centre and Institute for Southeast Asian Studies (ISEAS)-Yusof Ishak Institute. "The State of Southeast Asia: 2021 Survey Report." Last modified February 10, 2021. https://www.iseas.edu.sg/wp-content/uploads/2021/01/The-State-of-SEA-2021-v2.pdf.

11. Ibid

12. Lee, Liz. "Malaysia's Top Glove sees supply shortages boosting latex glove prices." Reuters, November 25, 2020. www.reuters.com/article/us-health-coronavirus-top-glove-supplies/malaysias-top-glove-sees-supply-shortages-boosting-latex-glove-prices-idUSKBN2850XX.

13. The White House. "Interim National Security Strategic Guidance." Last modified March 3, 2021. https://www.whitehouse.gov/wp-content/uploads/2021/03/NSC-1v2.pdf.

14. Ngor, Peng Bun, Kevin S. McCann, Gaël Grenouillet, Nam So, Bailey C. McMeans, Evan Fraser, and Sovan Lek. "Evidence of indiscriminate fishing effects in one of the world's largest inland fisheries." Scientific Reports 8, no. 8947 (2018). https://doi.org/10.1038/s41598-018-27340-1.

15. Scott, Katy. "Is Laos facing a dam disaster?" CNN, December 14, 2018, www.cnn.com/2018/12/14/asia/laos-hydropower-dams/index.html.

16. World Monuments Fund. "Ayutthaya and Other Flooded Sites." Last modified February 2019. https://www.wmf.org/project/ayutthaya-and-other-flooded-sites.

17. "World Heritage site under climate siege." ASEAN Post, September 2, 2018. www.theaseanpost.com/article/world-heritage-sites-under-climate-siege.

18. U.S. Mission to ASEAN. "Mekong-U.S. Partnership Joint Ministerial Statement." Last modified September 25, 2020. https://asean.usmission.gov/mekong-u-s-partnership-joint-ministerial-statement/.

19. Eyler, Brian, Alan Basist, Claude Williams, Allison Carr, and Courtney Weatherby. "Mekong Dam Monitor lifts the veil on basin-wide dam operations." Stimson, December 14, 2020. www.stimson.org/2020/mekong-dam-monitor-lifts-the-veil-on-basin-wide-dam-operations.

20. Participant notes from Stimson Center's Mekong-U.S. Partnership Track 15 Policy Dialogues with IUCN, March 15, 2021

21. Devlaeminck, David. "Timeline of the Lancang-Mekong Cooperation (LMC) Mechanism." Last modified February 2021. www.researchgate.net/publication/324678821_Timeline_of_the_Lancang_Mekong_Cooperation_LMC_Mechanism_Last_Updated_February_2021.

22. Myint-U, Thant. The Hidden History of Burma: Race, Capitalism and the Crisis of Democracy in the 21st Century. New York: W.W. Norton, 2020.

23. Vannarith, Chheang. "Fighting COVID-19: China's Soft Power Opportunities in Mainland Southeast Asia." Fulcrum, May 25, 2021. https://fulcrum.sg/fighting-covid-19-chinas-soft-power-opportunities-in-mainland-southeast-asia/.

24. Parameswaran, Prashanth. "Malaysia's Evolving Approach to China's Belt and Road Initiative." The Diplomat, April 23, 2019. https://thediplomat.com/2019/04/malaysias-evolving-approach-to-chinas-belt-and-road-initiative/.

25. Saludo, Ricardo. "When elephants fight, the grass gets trampled." Manila Times, September 24, 2020. https://www.manilatimes.net/2020/09/24/opinion/columnists/when-elephants-fight-the-grass-gets-trampled/771329.

26. Ahmed, Salman, Wendy Cutler, Rozlyn Engel, David Gordon, Jennifer Harris, Douglas Lute, Daniel M. Price, Christopher Smart, Jake Sullivan, Ashley J. Tellis, and Tom Wyler. "Making U.S. Foreign Policy Work Better for the Middle Class." Carnegie Endowment for International Peace, September 23, 2020. https://carnegieendowment.org/2020/09/23/making-u.s.-foreign-policy-work-better-for-middle-class-pub-82728.

27. Congressional Research Service. "Potential WTO TRIPS Waiver and COVID-19." Last modified June 16, 2021. https://crsreports.congress.gov/product/pdf/IF/IF11858.

28. DeYoung, Karen. "Samantha Power wants to restore U.S. prestige by getting American-made vaccines 'into arms' around the world." Washington Post, March 11, 2021. https://www.washingtonpost.com/national-security/samantha-power-usaid-vaccine-diplomacy/2021/05/10/69fd20d2-af7c-11eb-b476-c3b287e52a01_story.html.

29. Blinken, Antony J. "A Foreign Policy for the American People." Speech, Washington, DC, March 3, 2021. US Department of State. https://www.state.gov/a-foreign-policy-for-the-american-people/.

30. Greenblatt, Alan. "Fearing Trump's Trade Policies, U.S. States and Foreign Countries Grow Closer." Governing, January 23, 2018. www.governing.com/topics/mgmt/gov-governors-trade-foreign-diplomacy-trump-states.html/.

31. Barron, Laignee. "Malaysia's Mahathir Mohamad Will Become the World's Oldest Leader After a Shock Election Win." Time, May 10, 2018. www.time.com/5272113/mahathir-mohamad-defeats-najib-razak-malaysia-2018-election/.

32. Withers, Rachel. "What the Bloody Hell Just Happened in Australia?" Slate, May 20, 2019. www.slate.com/news-and-politics/2019/05/australia-election-upset-scott-morrison.html.

33. "Southeast Asian Leaders Address Regional Concerns Amidst Growing Major Power Tensions." Asian Politics and Policy 11, no. 3 (July 2019): 479-493. https://doi.org/10.1111/aspp.12476.

34. McMahon, Robert. "Can the State Department Bring More Diversity to the U.S. Diplomatic Corps?" Council on Foreign Relations, February 18, 2021. https://www.cfr.org/in-brief/can-state-department-bring-more-diversity-us-diplomatic-corps.

35. The Atlantic. "Yes, America Can Still Lead the World: Jake Sullivan and Jeffrey Goldberg in Conversation." January 18, 2019, video, www.americacanlead.theatlantic.com.

Sally Tyler is an attorney and policy practitioner in Washington, DC, where she has worked in the US labor movement for more than two decades. As an inveterate traveler and observer of politics and culture in Southeast Asia, she is a frequent commenter on events there and has presented at the International Conference of Asia Scholars. Her work has appeared in *New Mandala*, the Asia & Pacific Policy Society's *Policy Forum*, the *Mekong Review* and the *Washington Post*.